Kiss

Freedom

Goodbye

Kiss

Freedom

Goodbye

Views of a Concerned American

BY

CHERYL ROOTE

authorHOUSE®

AuthorHouse™
1663 Liberty Drive
Bloomington, IN 47403
www.authorhouse.com
Phone: 1-800-839-8640

First published by AuthorHouse   09/22/2011

ISBN: 978-1-4634-1721-5 (ebk)
ISBN: 978-1-4634-1723-9 (hc)
ISBN: 978-1-4634-1724-6 (sc)

Library of Congress Control Number: 2011910539

Printed in the United States of America

Chapter illustrations drawn and created by James Roote. April, 2011

This book is printed on acid-free paper.

Dedicated to my husband James Roote. His patience, understanding and support have been critical in organizing my thoughts for enlightening fellow Americans. His concerns and beliefs are as mine. Thank You Jim, for everything.

Kiss Freedom Goodbye was inspired by Glen Beck, Sarah Palin and many other great Americans who are concerned with the future of our Country and our well being.

~~~~~~~~Table of Contents~~~~~~~~

Preface

This is America, the land with the spirit of Santa Claus, the myth of the Tooth Fairy, the Easter egg hunts and all the holidays that put a glow in ones eyes and a hole in our pocketbook. This is the land of the free, the right to bear arms, the right to eat and think as we choose, and say what's on our mind.

What the Hell is going on? A President who we under estimated, when he said he would Fundamentally Transform America. What? How stupid of us not to see his plans for our future and his need to destroy America. How can he be a true American? Actually, rumor has it that his citizenship is in question.

Here is a man with high intelligence, a set mind and on a mission to turn our America upside down. Who raised and bred him to do and say the things he does? No President working for us, whether he is Democrat or Republican should be able to get away with the things he has. Why is this happening? Who is letting the pay offs slide by. Has the whole Democratic Party become corrupt?

It appears his mission is to break the United States, by putting us so far in debt, there is no way out. The spending must stop. Why and who, is responsible for the control of our future? Some one must stop this incredible scary journey into the jaws of Socialism and or Communism.

When our government doesn't take time to read the bills and reason with debate and good old Yankee ingenuity, how will we ever get out of this mess? It only takes three things to destroy us. Take away our right to bear arms will stop us from defending ourselves and our land. Take away our communications, and we have no way to seek help or know what's going on. Take away our money and we can no longer buy anything. Doesn't it look like that's what Obama is doing? How does he benefit from our losses and misery? Some how, he does.

What's in it for him? Who is actually controlling our world? Is the possibility of Communism approaching us in a very sly way? I for one do not look forward to loosing my rights. Being a very strong outgoing person will get me and thousands of others in trouble. We must stop the briberies, end the spending sprees, freeze prices and put an end to all the government raises and pork spending.

Being President is a lot of responsibility however it's like any other job. It's a job, and Obama is not doing his job correctly and should be put on a probationary period controlled by, we the people of the United States of America.

It's detrimental to our Nation to take over and hire a new Commander in Chief. This man will destroy America; we must stop his plans immediately. As his style, is to hurry up and sign the bills, we must hurry up and save our Nation. Freedom will be history, and the time will come to **Kiss Freedom Goodbye**...

The future will hold a severe change alright. You will not recognize our Nation as the land of the free. It will be more like the land of the doomed. People will be imprisoned for disagreeing with the political aspects of any kind of government decisions. You will be housed, fed, and owe your life to the government, much like old Russia, perhaps Germany at one time. As we all know that did not work out.

After some deep thought, I tried to figure out what party I was. I was raised a Democrat, but back years ago, the Democrats were the good guys, always trying to help the people. Times have changed. Am I now a Republican? I don't know, after seeing what their views and actions are, I tend to lean more toward the Conservative side.

But did you ever see anyone get into office if they were not Democrat or Republican? No. Those parties are to corrupt now and the pay offs they indulge in, are so deep that they tend to control way too much.

It's too bad that the job for Presidency has to be bought and paid for. It should be the right person for the job. Using myself as an example; I would take on the Presidential position. My organizational skills are exceptionally good. My ability to make decisions with a sound mind is far above average. The positions in my past have been managerial positions with many responsibilities, past and present experiences in owning a business and the ups and downs of success and failure. Selling and buying homes for rental properties and residential existence, the ability and stamina to face any situation that may arise. And the most important trait, which is needed right now, is honesty, trust and morals. Wouldn't you agree that those credentials are what we really need in the Whitehouse right now?

Although those credentials sound good, the fact that I am a female puts a strain on the attempt to succeed in the Presidential election. The second problem is of course money... It takes lots of money for campaigning. I don't care how good of person you are, if you don't have the money for running your campaign, you won't be able to run with the big dogs. Elections shouldn't be about money, but we all know that it is needed for advertisement to sell oneself.

So, I'll always be that diamond in the rough, who will never shine and put a sparkle of relief in America's downslide. Someone with money better step up to the plate and show a display of pureness, honesty and run for President and help our Nation.

Sarah Palin went a long ways in hers and McCain's campaign. I rooted all the way for her. She was an honest and real person. That is what's needed now to pull us out of this disaster. It is a crying shame that the press made things up about her and her family. I waited in line hours at one of her book signings, when I was told that no more people could get into see her. It broke my heart. Especially, when I had driven 150 miles the day before, to buy her book, because, it was to be in hand for the book signing. Then drove back 150 miles the next day to get turned down. But we all can't be lucky. I hope her speeches for the Tea Party reaches many Americans.

The most bothersome scam that takes place right in front of our eyes is the bribes. What is going on? If you want a Congressman's vote you pay him or her off. That's illegal. Why is this happening right in front of our eyes, and yet no one including Obama stops it. Since when do we do crimes out in the open, and its okay? This is not a good policy. It awes me to know that this is taking place. Let's arrest these people and carry on. Obviously crime does pay when it comes to Politics.

It's time to discuss our Nations bad habits. Stop the spending. Stop the Bribes. Stop the bail outs. Stop and read the bills, Stop the unwanted Health Care. Stop Cap and Trade and Stop any damn thing that's going to put our Nation in jeopardy. Most of all we must stop these crooks on Capital Hill including Mr. Obama.

Chapter 1 ....Obama's Stash

How many people have heard or seen this hilarious comment? It was a lady standing in line for money, believing that Obama was going to give everyone some money. And where was the money coming from? Obama's Stash....

What a riot! Could you believe that there are people out there that truly believe that President Obama is going to give them money so that they won't have to pay their house payments, car payments or buy food any more? Wow, what does he have them believing? I see him taking more and more from us and not giving us anything, especially money.

My theory is, get your ass out there and go to work and stop looking for hand outs. The government wants us at their mercy so they will have better control over us.

Does Congress really think that we the people are going to tolerate this? The Tea Party movement is a great source for us, the people to display our objections of government policies. So far they are calm and just want to be heard and understood. They want Congress to know that we are not happy. But... They don't seem to care. They are ignoring our every comment, our every action and the statements from the media.

Soon, things will not be so calm. The more they tax and take from us, the more rebellious the people will get. There will be no control over the people until the government gets control of themselves.

Maybe this Stimulus package is Obama's stash. No one really knows where all the money has gone. Trillions of dollars spent and yet very little to show for it. These bailouts are a joke, spending all that money to save a company that is just going to go belly up in a few months. Perhaps all this money is going into a special fund for Obama to use at a future date. Of course it will be used against us and not for us or to help us.

Where's the Tarp money? If the government would have given every taxpayer $100,000.00 with the ruling that it goes toward paying off each person's house payment and then their charge cards, everyone would be out of debt. The banks would get their money from the mortgage pay offs, giving them more money to lend and not have to count on the government to bail them out.

All charge card companies could lower their interest rates, making it more affordable to have a credit card, and have money flowing through the system again. Next, drop all prices 20% and put a price freeze on everything for a few years. This would strengthen the economy, putting faith in the Nations future and allowing people to live a life much deserved. Success is experienced through trial and error and perhaps failure. We can not let the government put us in a position where they make all the decisions. With the government buying out, many of the banks and car companies, this is wasting our money to further their take over. Our government does not need to buy companies out, this is not their job. If they were not trying to pull something over on us, then why are they purchasing all these companies, banks and acres and acres of land? Gottcha!

Let's face it, isn't someone's Stash, something they have hidden away. Is this where our Stimulus is going or perhaps to a bank in another Country? Maybe, to use for more pay-offs or bribes. After all, how many Presidential elections have you seen where the candidate buses young adults and bums to the polls? Or, have people guarding the polls, making scenes, beating up people because of their beliefs?

I am telling you something is wrong in Denmark. The whole election of 2008 was iffy. Many votes were bought and paid for. Just like the votes for this Health Care program. Promises made to certain states with funds from our Stimulus just to get their vote for Health Care, threats to Senators and Governors if they don't vote like Obama wants them to. This isn't legal. It isn't fair. Yet it keeps happening.

Wake up Americans, we must take action. How do we do that? We start by getting everyone that's in office now, OUT... We set term limits. No one stays in office long enough to learn the paths of evil. Getting to comfortable in a position allows an individual time to plot and scheme. We want honest reliable people. Men and women who want to keep America the land of the free and the craftiest ones of all. We police our own government. They will be accountable for all expenses. Money in and money out, we will know when and where it is going. We decide, we the people will decide who gets a so called bail out or help. A Republic/Democracy will arise again, but by us citizens, not the government.

Any stash that we find will be used to pay down our deficit. No more pork spending, you know, sneaking in 2 million for a new turtle highway or another 3 million for why sea gulls are gay. No more foreign contributions.

We are in trouble and should not be sending aid to other Countries making them one step up, when were so deep in debt ourselves. We take care of our poor before we take care of another Nation's poor or help them better their Nation. Charity begins at home, and by God, the United States of America is our Home.

I don't dislike Obama, however... I do not like the fact that he is running our Country into the ground and we can not trust his sneaky ways, I do not like the company he keeps or the company he used to keep. And most of all, we shouldn't trust trillions of dollars to someone who spends it unwisely. We are concerned for our future and our kid's future's. The more he spends the more money he prints. Our money will be like monopoly money, not worth anything. Then the Nation will suffer, because of him mishandling our funds. Money is the root of all evil. And now evil has embraced our Whitehouse. If Obama wants to spend foolishly, then he should dig into his own stash.

Chapter 2.......................... Health Care

It's hard to believe that against our wishes, we are getting Health Care shoved down our throats. The majority of Americans do not want a controlled health care system. I also believe this system will lead to death panels. Everything you hear about on the news really does make the death panel sound like a possibility. Congress is considering controlling the population, and not giving health care to older individuals. Since when do we control the life span of our population living within our Nation? Who the hell are they to decide how long we live? If it is up to the government, it sounds like they will not help with any medical problems if you are aging. Sure, Obama says he's not going to kill your grandma, and actually, he won't be killing her, just denying her a longer life.

Can this really be happening? Has the government flipped out? Are they going to live under the same rules as all of us Americans? Really, are they? How much do we really know about the Governor's, House and Senators after they are out of office? Do they get special benefits? They must, or they would be a little more apt to watch how they vote on these bills. If they have to live by the rules, then they would be more cautious when casting their votes. Sorry. I wasn't thinking. They don't read the bills. Majority of them have no idea what they are voting on. This is disgusting!

Obama demands urgency to the point of poor judgment for Congress to make a rational decision. And of course, if they don't vote the way Obama wants them to, then the bribes begin, and if it's not a bribe, it's a threat to either the state they represent or a member of the family will be in danger. This is against the law.

I truly think it is time to consider impeachment, perhaps a civil suit for mental stress, anxiety, or constant fear of the future of America etc. Everyday when I hear the news, I get tensed up, angry and can not figure out how the Whitehouse gets away with all that they do, right in front of our faces. It's a disgrace to our Nation!

This health care will present a shortage of Doctors creating longer waiting periods to see a Doctor. And because of taking so long to see a Doctor, our health will continue to get worse and perhaps cause death. Many Americans can not afford to pay for this insurance. Then to top it all off, if we don't pay for it, we get fined. I don't want any body controlling my health or when I can get help from a Doctor. Against the majority of the population, Obama and his sidekicks are forcing us to obey this much needed policy, per his own way of thinking. Rumor has it that some states don't have to have this Health Care plan. Just why can some people opt out and others can't? I guess it just depends on who you know or how much money you have.

Where will they get the money to pay for all this? I don't think they can raise our taxes enough to cover all these expenses without us working free for the government. Ah, that's the next step in their plan for controlling us.

Instead of a major Health Care Plan that we don't want and can't afford; we need to strengthen our Medicaid and Medicare programs. We need to combine the two together. Medicaid recipients receive better health care then Medicare recipients. This is not right. Medicaid is or was suppose to help those who had low income and or no job. Not monopolize the system to the point of having better coverage than the best there is out there. Although, we need to help individuals that need medical treatment, it should not be the ultimate plan. By combining the two together it would create less confusion and make more funds available for the seniors. Old age should not be a death threat. It should be a time when you can kick back and enjoy a little bit of life. After working all your life, it is crucial to have medical coverage. Of course it's not affordable, but that is why we have Medicare. The two year waiting period is ridiculous. I say do away with that. When retirement begins, so should your health benefits.

As we all know, that Medicare is almost broke. Gee, what did they do with all our money? People who have worked their whole life and paid their taxes will not be able to survive without their Social Security checks. Thanks to the government spending all of our medical savings, we could all be broke. Maybe that's what the government wants. We would be at their mercy and none of us want that.

A new plan should be implemented so that all F.I.CA payments go into a special bank account, of your own choosing. The money would not be able to be touched until retirement age. Of which, should be 65 for everyone. Then the total of all funds contributed through out your lifetime will be divided by 13 years, giving an average person living until they are 78 years of age. By dividing your total by 13 years, that would be your yearly income, then broken down to a monthly pay check that you would receive from the bank every month. As interest accrued, it would increase your monthly payments. If a person lives past the age of 78, then your monthly earnings would come from the deceased fund, which is the amount of money accumulated by individuals who expired earlier than the age of 78. It would all work out. It will guarantee retirement money for senior citizens to live on. And prevent the government from spending all the Social Security funds.

It's pretty bad we can't trust our own government. Gee, we can't even trust our President, because he does not listen to our wants or needs. The government needs to spend more time working on lowering medical costs and less time force feeding us with an expensive health care program. What about the illegal immigrants? How will health care be denied? A Doctor pledges to save lives, so how can he morally deny sick illegal individuals medical services?

Disability is also a problem through out the system. Once a person is granted their disability, there should be no waiting period or payment in the rears. You get paid from the day you get approved, and not from the day you applied.

Medicare needs to cover a tooth or teeth being pulled. If it wasn't necessary, you sure wouldn't be doing it for kicks. Too many people suffer from abscessed teeth and need them out. There must be coverage for these people. This is considered an emergency and must be considered for payment.

Our health care needs improvement, so when is Congress going to do this? Do all the members of the Whitehouse have the same coverage as us? Or, do they get a better health coverage than we do? If they are out of office, then they should be receiving the same Medicare as we do. If they did revert back to the care that we have, then perhaps more bills would be read more carefully.

We don't need government controlled abortions, controlled health care, death panels, control of our eating habits, our smoking habits, or control of anything to do with our body. We all know right from wrong. We know an apple is better than a candy bar. But our freedom should allow us to eat and do as we please.

Taking away our rights in any part of our existence should be against the law. We as individuals and humans have the right to choose. We may not choose the right path, but it's the path that we, as Americans have chosen.

Prescription coverage is also very important, and should be part of our Medicare program. Seniors can not afford some of these drugs. Why should they have to choose between eating dinner or buying their medications? Especially, when you see the members of Congress waste our money on stupid trivial things, while others struggle to exist. Where does share the wealth come in when this situation is among the needy?

When it comes to disability pensions, there are a lot of people who scam the system. This of course ruins it for those who are disabled. A person would get more on disability than they would if they received their regular Social Security check. Giving more reasons for a dishonest person to come forward and try to trick the system. Anyone becoming disabled from the age of 50 or older should automatically begin to collect their retirement money. This would decrease government costs and prevent people from claiming disability just before retirement age of 62 or 65. Whether a person is retired or disabled, there should be no difference in their income or benefits. Living on a fixed income is hard to do. Everyone knows that your health begins to go down hill by the age of 60.

Another disgusting medical problem is VA hospitals. Our military men and women risk their lives for our Country and do not need the hassle's of getting health care through a VA hospital. Have you ever experienced a trip to a VA hospital? They treat you like you have the plaque. They are rude, uncaring and disorganized. This of course is a government run facility. The best thing for our Veteran's, would be to close down all of these hospitals. Let our Veterans choose whom they want to see and where they want to go.

They should be able to show a Veteran's ID card at any hospital or clinic and be cared for. These VA hospitals are not plentiful, so you usually have to drive a very long ways to get to one. And of course, there is always a return trip back. The money spent for gas alone, would break a person. There is no excuse for the way our Veterans are treated and cared for. It would actually cost the government less money. There would be no employee's, building maintenance, rent, utilities and no insurance. They would not have to pay for Doctors or Nurses. All the way around this would be cheaper. It's amazing how simple this sounds, yet the government does not try to cut costs.

Our President should be looking out for our best interest, instead of running up the bills so bad that we are in debt for the rest of our lives. Our poor children will have hell to pay. We must take control back from the government by any means possible to strengthen America and revive its reputation as a free Nation.

What will happen to people who can't afford health care? Why is it that some people will not be covered? Is this fair to all? Will some have to pay for those who can't pay? These questions need answers, and yet we get none. The healthiest thing for all of America is to get everyone in office now, Out. So please America watch how you vote. Aim to get rid of the crooks in our political system.

Any elections coming up will be the most important decisions you will have ever made. Not only for health care sake, but our future and our children who will build the future. There are many of you out there that are not paying attention to what's going on. Wake up, or tomorrow will bring a surprise of bad news and lost rights.

You will see a life style that you will not like and you will wonder what the hell is going on? It will be too late, once you have realized that your life is not what it use to be and never will be again. Then depression will set in, anger will rise, patience will diminish and trouble will haunt the Country. This sounds a little dramatized, but what if it's true? Let's not take a chance. We can do something to prevent this now. Now is when we must take a stand and fight for our rights.

Majority of the population does not want health care that is run by the government. We all know that it will hurt the economy and perhaps bankrupt America. It is speculated that it will cost over 2 trillion dollars. You know that it will cost even more, because our lawmakers never get it right. Their figures are always off. Imagine that, we elect these people into office and they can't even add or subtract as well as we can. But we all know that we can fix this when we clean house at election time.

Why is it that some states are getting help with medical costs and others are not? Look at Vermont, Mass, Florida and Conn., they are getting billions of dollars for either medical centers or help with Medicare. Let's not forget Louisiana, and the help they will receive for Medicare. It is not fair that these states get special deals and other states do not.

This Health Care Bill has about 2300 pages of corrections and fixes. To top it all off, when a speed reader is hired to read it, he states that it is some what confusing because it makes references to other areas in the bill and when you go to that spot, there is nothing there that pertains to what you just read. What a mess. So now we have a bill that they voted yes on and it can not be understood. That is pretty sick if you ask me. It is pitiful to think that we trust in our lawmakers and they screw it up so bad.

This Health Care bill has many extras that they have set 5 billion dollars aside for. It's a Public Health Fund for preventative maintenance on our bodies. They hope to provide healthy activities such as building new playgrounds and jungle gyms, adding more bicycle paths and parks. By adding more sidewalks they are hoping for us to do more walking. Also opening farm markets for fresh produce. We are being made to exercise and do more extra curricular activities to better our health. Since when is it up to the government to control our activities and force us to buy something we don't want. If they can get away with this, it's just a matter of time before they are making us do something else we don't want to.

They are really pushing our buttons. I don't think that is a good idea, for them to get to pushy with us Americans. We all know that trouble is brewing and it is very scary.

They keep saying that we will save money with this bill. But do you really believe this? It is impossible to save money, let alone make any money. It is going to bankrupt us to the point of no return. Obama is incorrigible, he does not listen to us and could care less if we like his ideas or not.

Soon Obama will hire someone to be a Medicare bounty hunter. This person will catch waste and fraud in the health care system. He hopes to cut costs and save 2 billion dollars. He could cut a lot more costs if he just did away with all the wasteful spending as mentioned in chapter 17. That will be a whole lot more than 2 billion dollars.

By the year 2019 there will be an extra 30 million Americans on this Health Care program. Now please tell me how we can afford this? You do the math. It just isn't going to happen.

Many Doctors are dropping Health Insurance in droves, making the patients handle the billing of insurance. This is not good. The Doctors are objecting to this Health Care Program and some are considering leaving the states because of it. We do not need to loose our good Doctor's due to our new Health Care System. Because there will be a shortage of Doctors, our politicians are considering us seeing a Nurse instead of a Doctor. We will not feel comfortable knowing that a Nurse does not have the knowledge of a Doctor. So for many of us, our health could be in jeopardy.

Did you know, one out of four Doctors, order expensive tests because they are scared of lawsuits? It is too bad that people are so sue happy. They are just looking for some quick cash and what an easy way to get it. That's why we need to put a stop to these frivolous law suits. The more test ordered, the more our insurance goes up. If no insurance is available, then that person has to pay for all these extra tests, just because the Doctor fears law suits.

Are you aware that the Muslim's living in our Country will not have to have Healthcare? They also do not have to pay any of the fines involved if they do not have Healthcare. Why is this? We should be concerned with these Muslim's coming into our Country and having so many options that they can demand we follow their religious beliefs and laws.

This is our Country and these foreigners come here and they get treated better than us. This disgusts me to no end. But it is obvious that Obama caters to everyone but us Americans, gee I wonder why? What is he?

Rumor has it that Obama was carrying and reading the book named; The Past American World. This book is about the U.S. dissolving and turning to a Global government and being controlled by said government. This bothers me and should bother everyone reading this book. We must repeal this Healthcare and all other bills that Congress is considering that would tamper with our freedom.

Health care has become more of a political issue as opposed to a medical issue.

It appalls me to think that a government official has the last say so when it comes to our health. Doctor's should have the final decisions on what we as individuals need to better our health. The government has intercepted the medical profession and now rules the roost. The fee's that a Doctor's office charges us is ridiculous and soon will be controlled by our wonderful politicians.

I called my Doctor to make an appointment for a cyst like tumor I found in my arm that had been bothering me for over a month. I had to wait two weeks for an appointment.

In the mean time, I came down with a sore throat and had a rash on my leg. So I figured I would talk to the Doctor about all three things. When finally sitting in the room waiting for my Doctor, he walked in ask me about my arm. He assured me it was nothing to worry about and started to leave the room. I said excuse me there are a couple other things I want to say. He then stated that he was very busy and behind and he did not have time for any other health issues other than what I came in for. This really made me mad.

I was charged $121.00 for a 4 minute chat and still was unable to address my other two problems. Just what the hell is going on in our Country? This disgusts me to no end also.

When we have to pay for services that are half assed, then things need to be changed.

Then to top it all off, a few months later I receive a letter from my Doctor telling me that his time is limited and that during my future visits I must limit my health problems to one problem that is bothering me the most because they do not have time to address more than one problem. What the hell is that all about? Since when do we as patients have to hold back on our health problems? I was so angry about this letter. I could not believe the audacity of such a ruling. What kind of Doctor's office would send out such a letter? I have been seeing this doctor for years. This tends to show us what the future holds in regards to our health care.

So now that they have shoved this health care bill down our throats, I am sure things will get worse as time goes on. It is time that we Americans stand up for our rights and demand the respect that is due us.

Now that the Republicans are more plentiful in office, they are going to repeal this Health Care Bill. This needs to be done. We do not, and I repeat, we do not need the government controlling our health problems. Of course Harry Reid will try to block all votes on the repeal of Obama Care because the Democrat's want it left alone. We know that this was Obama's big project and no matter how much Congress does repeal it, there will still be doubts that Obama will sign. He more than likely will veto any bill that is directed toward his Health Care Bill.

With the Health Care Bill being such an important issue, I see many Judges ruling that it is against the Constitution to push this Health Care Bill on us. Gee, it's kind of nice to see that someone in the government is actually doing their job. It is about time that someone is taking the Constitution to heart. Just maybe things about Health Care will turn out in our favor. But it seems like every time they do make something right, then they do three more things wrong to harm or distress us.

Although it was nice to see they voted against the End of Life Counseling. This was kind of a morbid subject. Who wants to get counseling on dying? A sick person knows when their life is coming to an end, and I feel sure that subject would like to be put on the back burner and not thought about and be reminded that soon your life will be over, so lets talk about the end result. What's the matter with Congress? Are they running out of things to ruin our life with?

Our Medicare system works well for us, it is a crying shame the government has to mess with it. What is wrong with bettering it to some degree and let it be. There are so many other places that expense's can be cut. They should start cutting expense's at the Whitehouse before they touch Social Security and Medicare. Concessions need to be made but not with these two issues. We need to leave the police and military alone also.

We need to cut all these trivial grants and minimize Medicaid or better yet, do way with it. Our government does not pay attention to detail or they would know that there are so many other areas that need to be done away with. But oh no, we citizens don't know anything.

Thanks to Michelle Obama, our children are going to be told how to eat and parents will be in trouble if the children don't eat like she wants them to. Michelle wants to improve nutrition in America to fight childhood obesity. After all, the parents don't know how to feed their kids. Soon the schools will be forced to serve things that Michelle says the schools can serve. Many schools will now offer salad bars in their cafeterias.

Michelle has even partnered up with Wal-Mart to get produce prices lowered so it is more affordable to buy the healthier foods. The only thing good about this is, that produce prices will go down. The bad side of all this is, here is just one more thing in our life that they want to take control of. The only reason the government wants a health care program is so that they can tell us what we can eat or can't. The excuse will be, since they are providing health care, they have the right to tell you what to eat to keep you as healthy as possible so you don't cost them any more money. It's all just a scam. They really don't care if we are healthy or not. They really don't give a damn about us. They just want to hold their positions of power and receive their big fat pay checks.

Do you know that someone wants to ban male circumcisions? My goodness, Why? The male gender has had this done for many years because it has proven to be a hygiene matter and is better for the males. Someone probably thought this one up so when the Health Care Plan goes into affect, the government won't have to pay for it. It's like they don't want to pay for women to have mammograms either. There have been many women that have conquered cancer because of these mammograms.

This is very important to the female gender. We must wonder who comes up with all these bad ideas.

Speaking of sexual gender, have you heard about the children's books out now that describe sexual intercourse and show illustrations on how to do so? Some things just need to be left alone until the time is right. Why are we submitting this kind of teachings to children? Let's face it, sex is not a secret but you would like to at least spare a child from knowing all about it at such a young age.

Chapter 3 .... Changes

When campaigning for the Presidential election was taking place we all hoped to see some changes. It was important to each and everyone for that to happen. However, the change that America was hoping for, and the change that we got were not what we had in mind. Obama made many promises. But he never carried through with them. Leaving us frustrated. When Obama stated that he was going to fundamentally transform America, we did not read in between the lines. He not only is transforming us into an insecure nation, but he is drowning us in debt. His popularity vote is decreasing. How can we have confidence in a man who hires felons to work in the Whitehouse? It appears that he is not working for us, but against us. His actions don't come across like a true American. It's like he is a plant from another Country, plotting to destroy and conquer.

We must ask ourselves if this truly is the right man for the job. I personally do not think he is. I think it's scary to watch him put us in jeopardy. Why are his dealings always behind closed doors? Everything this man has to say should be public except for Homeland Security issues. Why are the Democrats allowed to discuss anything without the Republicans present? What kind of Democracy is this? Anything that our President has to say to the Democrats must also be for the Republicans to hear. Without this, meeting of the minds then we are not a Democracy. It is unconstitutional for only one party to be involved and not both. It is important that Obama goes through the normal Congressional process, why should he be any different than other Presidents?

It's hard to trust a man that secretly hides behind closed doors with a select few, including his Czars. These Czars bother me to the point of wanting an explanation of just what is going on. No one should be able to only report to the President. This is no different then having a shadow government. This is sneaky dealings. It should not be allowed and we should question why he is able to get away with this. Especially, when, the majority of these Czars are Felons, Communist, Socialist, Liberals and the undesirable. Why does Obama need so many Czars? No other Presidents have had Czars. It's like he has his own mini secret government on the side lines. This is strange to say the least.

We wanted change. So be careful what we wish for, we might just get it. We did want change, but not a change to our lifestyle, or our pocketbook, and most of all not our rights being infringed upon. Hoping for change to better our society is a given. We don't want the kind of change Obama has in mind for us.

One change that is recognized more so now than ever, is our politicians don't bother to read the bills before signing them. Did we elect a bunch of idiots into office?

Since when do you sign anything that you haven't read? Any politician that has his signature on a bill and doesn't know what was in it should be released from office. It definitely is not the person I want representing us or our Nation.

Millions of people are counting on Congress to make good decisions for us, and the fact that they don't take the time to read the bills just grinds my ass. This is why our Nation is sinking.

The pork spending must stop, but yet it continues to show up in these bills. Why do we even have a House of Representatives or a Senate? They are useless crooks.

We the people are getting wise to them now, so all you politicians better clean up your act or you will join the ranks of the unemployed.

Does the phrase, Redistribute the Wealth, sound familiar? Do you honestly know a person with money that wants to share it? No. Obama wants to take from the wealthy and give to the poor. Robin Hood no longer exists. This is perhaps wishful thinking on Obama's part. Another great theory in this new political scam is to step down. Now, you tell me, who in hell wants to give up their money, step down from their power, and be completely happy that they did that. The only way that is even possible, is if Obama pass's a law, making this happen. Just maybe Obama and his Czars should step down and let someone run this Country that can get us out of this mess he has created. This would be a change that majority of the population would favor.

Speaking of population, just what step will be taken to control population? They seem to be concerned with controlling the population and considering government controlled abortions. Is this what we have to look forward to? What if you already have four children and you are pregnant again, and the government says No you can't have this child. You must abort it. I know for a fact that this will not go over to well with Americans. Just recently, I heard on TV about controlling the population by genocide. Do we now have to watch our food intake because we don't know what's being put in it? What about our drinking water? Also the flu and swine vaccine's that we are urged to get. Have they been laced with chemicals for population control? This sure does make you wonder just who you can trust, after all the government will have to decrease the population of our Nation in order to have better control of us.

This isn't good when we have to tip toe through life wondering what the government has in store for us next. Things never were an issue until just lately. Why do you suppose this is? Is there a private society out there that Obama and others are members of and consist of powerful people that want to take over the World? A World leader has been mentioned several times. I see no benefit for a World leader. There are too many of us for a World leader to control or lead, perhaps, that's why controlling the population is such an important factor. We do not want or need a Global government.

There are many changes that would be healthier than some of their ideas to control population. Mandatory birth control would be better than poisoning our food and water. Changes are needed to further future existence however they must not be to the degree of harming or alarming us as American citizens. I really feel that Americans will only take so much before they rebel. We should hope this never happens, but I fear that the government is trying to push us past our limits. We all have our own limits, so we will just hope for the best. Some one rich and more powerful over rules our government. Who might that be?

The first thing I would do if I were to walk into the Whitehouse tomorrow and be responsible for the position of Presidency would be to stop all spending. Not one check or cash would leave the building. I want to see the National Debt Board come to a complete stop. Then no money would go out with out looking at each expense to determine if we need to discontinue or cut back on this particular debt. This is what needs to be done to save our Country.

All grants would be put on hold. All Foreign Aid would be stopped. Not one dime would go to another Country. Obama states that the foreign aid sent to these other Countries is for peace and security, but since when do we have to pay someone to be nice to us? This probably hurts us worse than any pay out in the Whitehouse. I would deny any raise's for any government official. All paid vacations would be put on hold. All government officials would no longer have any thing paid for out of our budget. It would have to come out of each officials own pocket.

There would be cut backs such as lighting in the Whitehouse. Many rooms are not used and yet they remain lit up. This is a waste of our money. We could save thousands of dollars just by turning light switches off. We can cut 25% of the Whitehouse staff and members such as Czars. No more luxuries for any reason would be allowed.

There would be no more donations to charities. All Stimulus packages would become null and void. Obama is even considering another Stimulus package. This is crazy; this guy thinks our money never runs out.

All Whitehouse and government buildings that need yard work would be put up for lower bids. We know this could be done and save many dollars. The same would apply for other services that are needed by the Whitehouse.

Air Force One would not be used except for the President and only if it was a must and very important. No more flying Michelle Obama around and Pelosi and all the others who are using and abusing the Whitehouse services. They will have to pay for their own plane tickets out of their pockets.

Obama stated in his State of the Union speech that he wants us to have high speed trains, perhaps to enhance our growth and try to out do the Joneses, if you know what I mean. Here is another example of poor planning and putting us further in debt. We must first get a handle on our debt and more control of our future before we try to out do other Countries. We need to be thinking about the survival mode of our Nation, not trying to out do or better someone else. It is better for the United States to be well off and in control of our Nation than to venture out and keep spending money in hopes of it making us look good.

The pork spending would come to an end. Obama keeps saying there will be no more. But he ignores the pork when it's in a bill. Well no more of that. If any pork is in a bill I would automatically veto the bill. Congress would finally get the hint and quit doing it.

Could you imagine all the millions and even billions that we could have back if we cut out all the outrageous spending that is mentioned in Chapter 17? Why it would put our Social Security back into a safer mode and less worries on our seniors as they age.

There is no end to what I could do to cut our costs and get us back on the right track. If I am confident that this can be done, then please tell me why someone is not doing this in our government? I can tell you why, they do not want to have to cut back and take concessions. They like being able to blow our every dollar and will continue to do so.

One day the right person is going to step on all their toes and slap their hands and say "No more dipping into the cookie jar guys, your done." Until that day comes we are basically screwed. Our debt will be the death of us all.

There is no end to all the changes that can be done and all the services that can be discontinued. This would be a job in its self, just trying to control Congress from spending millions and billions of our tax payer's dollars.

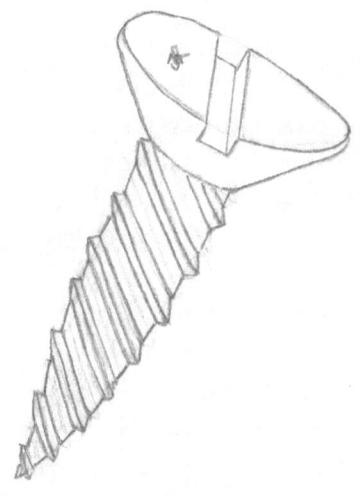

Chapter 4 .... Taxes

A nyone who receives a paycheck knows how much less they are receiving because of taxes. With the health care system being pushed on us, how will we afford to pay the extra taxes? Then, they are considering a fat tax, carbon tax, tanning tax, and several other taxes that they are going to demand. Soon we will be working for nothing, paying our whole paycheck to the government. This is no way to help America out when the economy is on a downslide. I can hear the government saying: "Heh, let's tax the people more money, so we can waste more money on bail outs, payoffs, and bribes." Congress probably wants more vacation pay, and of course raise's. Why should any one in Congress get a raise when the American people are struggling to make ends meet? We need to make them take concessions to benefit our

Country and strengthen the economy. Our take home pay sucks.

Because the government needs more money they are trying to tax anything and everything. Can you believe they want to put tax on insurance premiums? Wow, talk about digging deep to find more reasons to get our money. Why are they allowed to wheel and deal with the Unions and others who do not have to pay certain taxes? These double standards have to go. Do you realize that General Electric made over 14 billion dollars and did not have to pay any taxes? Why is this? They also received a bail out with some of the Tarp money. We struggle to pay our taxes on a small pay check of $300.00 and yet G.E. doesn't have to. We must get new people in to office and resolve this mess that Obama and his sidekicks have created.

We need to do away with State taxes. Any money needed by the state should be gotten from the government. Each state receives funds now, so why is it broken down to us paying state taxes. As mentioned in a prior chapter, no more F.I.C.A. taxes will be taken by the government for Social Security. Those funds will be deposited in a retirement account per your choice of bank. We need to get rid of all city taxes. Why should you have to pay taxes to work in one city and not other's. This is just another tax goody the government has managed to sneak in.

The only tax coming out of a person's paycheck should be Federal income tax. It should be a set amount, like a flat tax, such as 20% of your check. So that individuals can figure out their own paycheck and know what to expect on each pay week. It should not be a higher tax if you are single. That's penalizing you for not being married. By taxing 40% on your 53rd paycheck is garbage. You are again being penalized for doing well and receiving a bonus check or even an extra vacation check. This kind of control leaves it impossible for people to strive to do better and work harder. Another tax problem is double taxation. When you receive a refund at the end of the year because you paid in too many taxes, then you also have to claim that as income and get taxed on it again. Where does Uncle Sam get off by doing that? Why do we have to pay taxes on our refunds? This is another gottcha tax that the government needs to get rid of.

There are other channels the government could take, for them to receive more help from us as taxpayers. Such as, charging a higher tax on luxury items which would be a Value Added Tax, whether it is a cell phone, TV, DVD player, boats, snowmobiles, etc. We don't want to have to pay more taxes, but now that the deficit is so high, we have to pay it down some how. Lotteries were supposed to help school funding. So what happened to all the money? Someone put their fingers in the cookie jar on this one. There should have been enough money from lottery sales to take care of every school out there and help pay down the deficit. But now the schools are in trouble and they want to quit busing our children and make them pay for their own school supplies. Eventually that won't be enough help for them either. Leave it to our government to mess up the school system. What does our government do with all this money? It's time for all the spending that the Whitehouse does, be posted so that we can see what's being spent on what? It is time for Americans to have a helping hand and be involved in where all the monies go? We also should be able to vote on what the government wants to spend and how much they are allowed to spend.

When it comes to our seniors, there should be no earned income ceiling on their wages. If they choose to work after retirement, the choice should be theirs without worrying about making to much money and getting their Social Security cut or taken away. Because they have paid taxes all their life, their income after retirement should be tax free. There is no reason why we do not take better care of our senor citizens who have worked all their lives. Most seniors feel too badly or are to sick to work. So it's not like they would take over too many jobs. If they can do the job at 75 or 80, then more power to them. The government acts like old age is a disease and don't find it necessary to give seniors help.

Another tax I find appalling is school taxes. Why should an adult who has no children or their children have grown up and moved out of the house, have to pay school taxes? Once a child is out of the home, then the school taxes should have to be discontinued. The parents have paid more than their share of taxes through out the 18 years of child rearing. It is only right that these taxes stop. I am sure the majority of people will agree with this.

The importance in doing a yearly tax return is necessary, however why do we have to pay for this service? Tax preparation charges are terrible. You practically have to get a loan to have them done. This should be a service that the government offers to us as an American citizen. This is something that Washington needs to consider. We are being charged to balance out year end taxes. The tax codes are too complicated for the average American to do them. What a bunch of bull. People are tired of not having enough money to live on and yet work everyday, for what?

Wouldn't it be nice if you could just once in awhile take a paycheck and buy something that you may need? Maybe a new alarm clock or a new coffee maker or perhaps pay to have your carpet cleaned. That's why the majority of people are in charge card debt. Too many things in life pop up. In one week alone, the battery on your vehicle goes dead, your spouse gets an abscessed tooth and needs a Dentist, and you need to fill a prescription. So we grab the old charge card just to survive the week. This totals to about $400.00. How many times can that Visa or MasterCard take a hit like that? But too many of these things happen in a year and before you know it, you are in debt up to your elbows. You don't make enough money to pay it off so now the interest rates are eating you alive as you struggle to pay more and more of your bills.

Gee, let's thank the government for this also. Making deals with the charge card companies and setting a time frame just long enough for them to raise all the interest rates. Now your payments are higher and the chances of getting it paid off are zilch. Why isn't the government putting an interest freeze on these companies? They are allowing us to swim in debt. Yes, it is our fault that we spent the money. But circumstances arise and what the hell is a person suppose to do? If taxes continue to rise like the government says they will, then we can hang it up, because the struggle to survive will be impossible.

We need to ask the question, why does the government push us to our limits? They should try living on what most of us have to live on. No body can budget money better than a family struggling to make ends meet. Thank God for the dollar stores. If you don't shop there, then shame on you. Too bad there isn't a dollar grocery store. It would be very busy and a big success.

If the government would just stop spending and wasting our money, perhaps they would not have to tax us so much. This is a big problem. Someone must get into office and step on a few toes and make some adjustments. The possibility of this happening real soon is probably going to be difficult. We all want our rights and our freedom, along with the money we earn. With out help, we can **Kiss Freedom Goodbye.**

This isn't hard to figure out so what's the problem? What good is it to ask questions with boldness if they are ignoring us? We might as well be talking to a brick wall. That is really scary. Only idiots could feel comfortable not answering our questions, or giving reasons for their actions, which says, that they could care less about you and me. We are just a grain of sand in a mountain of dirt.

It is amazing that approximately 36% of the population does not pay taxes. That is over one third of the United States. It just does not seem fair to those of us who are paying our taxes.

The government is trying to get as much money as they can out of us through different taxes. They want to increase the Capital Gains tax, however we all know that is not going to help by much. It is just a matter of time before they will raise all our taxes. As you recall, Obama said he would not raise our taxes. It's just another one of his lies.

It is strange the way Congress is picking and choosing which items to tax. In the state of Maine they want to put a tax on blueberries. Come on. This is a healthy item, and now they want to tax it. They are more confused than can be imagined. On the other hand they want to tax noise makers in W. Virginia. Gee do you think all the money we get from that tax will help our debt? In Washington D.C. they want to tax the grocery bags used to put your groceries in. What next? Oh Yes, in the state of Illinois they are going to tax snicker bars but not twix because twix have flour in them. Do you realize that this fat tax is really just a power move on the government's part? The more control they can enforce upon us, the more power it gives them to run our lives.

For all you beer drinkers in the state of Washington, the Governor wants to triple the taxes on beer. It is nice to see that they are starting to pick on alcohol for awhile instead of tobacco.

Now that the government has made Health Care a right and they are controlling it, they are going to put all sorts of taxes and stipulations on any kind of food that may be bad for us, such as junk food. This will give them the power to tell us what we can eat. But we all know it's not about our health. It's about them having power over us and being able to tax us more and take away our freedom.

They say that junk food is just as addicting as crack cocaine. Although I have never tried crack cocaine, I tend to disagree with this kind of thinking. If we eat 5 candy bars, I know we can't get high off them or hurt someone or ourselves. Who possibly could have compared these

2 things and come up with something so stupid? At one point in time they did an experiment with rats and kept giving them electric shock treatments to get them to quit eating junk food, but the rats still continued to eat it. So now we are being led to believe that junk food is addicting. The truth is that the government will now tax the hell out of any thing and every thing because they are in trouble and the people of the United States are going to have to pay for it.

We are all familiar with Cap & Trade, which is also called Climate Tax or Energy Tax. But are you all aware of the outrageous price we will incur if this goes into affect? There are independent environmental scientist that say this will do zero for the environment. Why is the government even considering such a tax or raising our fuel cost? Now they are also thinking about a Carbon Tax. Did you ever think you would see the day that it would cost you to breathe?

The Green technology ways are so expensive, and will take years to recover your money back, let alone bettering the environment. We need to concentrate on developing a smoother economy, which will help out with the Green jobs and technology.

We should have one tax only like a flat tax across the board. Then we need to make sure that Congress can not raise any taxes on us. We will implement a tax freeze. But we have to vote the right people in to office.

Obama says he wants to help small businesses, but he has hiked the taxes up on Federal, Capital Gains and Investment Income. What kind of help is that? The tax cuts that Bush put into effect have expired. Obama was reluctant in renewing them but says he will not renew them again. Guess what happens to us when it expires? Yes, taxes will soar through the roof. He also has increased the Medicare Payroll Tax. As we are learning more about Obama and all his help, don't you want to just slap him?

Did you hear that the UAW is suing GM for employee health care costs? It's only 450 million dollars. Of course we the people have to pay to fight this law suit. Who owns GM now? Right, so we are suing ourselves. What a mess. Is this just another tactic to shuffle more of our money around so that it looks like we spent it? This is a really good trick. I do give them credit; they sure are sly crafty bastards. It will be a relief when Obama leaves office. We Americans don't like the closed door policy that he implements every time he wants to play let's cut a deal. How crooked does this seem to you?

We all know our future is going to be rugged. We will be taxed to the max and expected to live with it. Right now, the citizen's of America are pretty fed up. We all tend to feel like were being used and abused. We don't like it. It makes us feel helpless and angry.

The government states that taxes are what we pay for a civilized society. Do you think that fraud, waste, failed policies, lies and productive citizens being taxed to death is a civilized society? What a joke. Actually there is nothing civilized about our government. Right now I don't think society quite knows what to think or do about the policies that are being forced upon us. Time will soon tell.

Now that the government is in a financial mess they state they must do some creative tax cuts. Have you ever seen them be creative with any policies? The only thing that Congress creates is more problems.

Chapter 5.......................................Ideas

The path to our future is made of ideas. We all have a vision that we would like to see come true. Some are trivial and some are detrimental to the function of society. To further a better smoother operating system we need to take ideas of individuals and sort through them for solving long term problems. We need to reward those that can come up with ideas to better us or our Country. Many minds are better than one or several. So why not offer a monetary reward for those individuals who can come up with ideas to things such as, terrorism, war, health care, cutting costs etc. This gives people initiative to strive to solve worldly problems and gives them some extra cash in their pockets.

   First example of a real problem in our Country is poverty and the homeless. It would be costly for the government to take care of all these individuals. I recommend that we make better use of our prisoners. We need a wider distribution of food supply. So we must put the prisoners to work in gardens. In warmer climate states, they can grow vegetable gardens all year long. You take a person who is in prison for growing marijuana. It is very hard to grow plants of any kind without some botanical knowledge. A marijuana grower has probably the best green thumb out there. So we put him in charge of our vegetable gardens. The prisoners can take care of the crops, pick the crops and then all veggies can be shipped to designated cities for the homeless. There is no end to what we could grow and reap. How beneficial this would be to help out our poorer citizens and our seniors. We must punish the law breakers Yes, but why not use them to prevent poverty and starvation. These prisoners have skills that we could use for many things instead of letting them rot behind bars.

One way to stop people from dumping their old dryers, washers, dishwashers and many appliances out on a secluded dirt road, would be to stop charging us citizens' to get rid of our appliances. Let's face it, if it is of no use to you anymore and it does not work, why would you want to pay to get rid of it? These charges must stop. It would better the environment. Why not, take these appliances to a waste dump and once a month they would be picked up and taken to a place where our prisoners who are mechanically inclined, could fix them and then they can be distributed to the needy. This also would lessen the waste in our landfills. Americans have a lot of waste and it is important to recycle some of our waste products. The prisoners could really be helpful to those in need.

Our prisons are over crowded now so why not use the people with less criminal offenses like tickets, child support and probation breakers, for a program like Community Punishment Aides. These offenders would wear a tether around their ankles and have to be in their homes by a certain time, to prevent breaking a said sentence. Each offender would be assigned to the city of which they live in. Each day a different business would request them for the day or a few hours, to do things like sweeping, cleaning, dusting, and shoveling or whatever that business would like done. All business owners could use someone extra to help out with things but can't always afford to pay more wages for help. This would be an embarrassing situation for the offender and perhaps teach him not to break the law.

It costs too much money to put people in jail. Another solution is definitely needed to resolve over populated prisons. There are always some who can't be trusted with this kind of program, for these individuals a stricter more guarded set up would be assigned.

Help is needed in all aspects of life, whether you are a homeowner, business owner or a single parent. Someone, some where always needs a helping hand.

There are certain programs that could use some adjustments. As an example, parents of assistant programs who receive food stamps, they are allotted way too much money for food. I have known and seen many people trying to sell or wheel and deal with their food stamps/card. Their cupboards are fuller than an individual that works for a living.

This program could save costs by cutting back on the amount issued. On the other hand, our seniors could use some help with food. I am not talking about powdered milk and eggs or a box of cheese. They need fruits and vegetables and meats. If we had some of the programs I have suggested, than this would help. Meat can come from wild game also. Just recently there have been programs that offer wild game. However this is not plentiful enough to help our seniors.

Are you people that make some of these rules forgetting that some day you will be old and needy? I am beginning to wonder just how far in this thought process that these decisions makers are thinking. When people are receiving assistance, it should not be to the degree of living a luxurious life style, but to fill in the gaps of needy areas until you get back on your feet. Too many people get to comfortable in this easy way of living and do not try to get ahead or go out looking for work. This is making people lazy and unappreciative. Making the hard working individual a little jealous and irate.

Instead of our government cutting cost in our military, they should be modernizing our military. We need to be the best we can be, even if it cost more money. After all, look at all the money they have wasted that could have gone for a better more prepared military. When it comes to our military, we should not be cutting cost or cutting back. This is our life line. They defend us and fight for our rights. We need our military, so why is Obama weakening it? I would love Obama to answer that question. It seems Obama's policies are reckless, and he just can't get it right. Americans can tolerate a lot, but enough is enough when it comes to Obama's policies. This war with Libya is costing us millions of dollars. Sorry, I forgot Obama is not calling this war. He is calling it a Kinetic Military Action. He is only calling it this because it was a way for him to dodge Congress and their approval of this. Again it's just more of our money going down the drain.

It appears Al Gore is not giving up with his global warming idea. He is now going into the schools with a program called Inconvenient Youth; he is working on our children. This is something we don't want. We do not need someone convincing our children that the world is in trouble and they need to help out. Our children do not need this burden on their shoulders. Some children could take this to heart and become upset. Worse yet, they will come home to us parents and preach to us what they learned in school. Then if you don't believe them they will not think very highly of you, because that's what their learning in school. If there is a global warming in the future, the green philosophy that they are trying to instill into us will not be enough help to stop the problem. It will be more of a waste of money and time. Our money and our time, it will be useless when it comes to Mother

Nature. We should not believe that mankind is hurting our atmosphere and environment. It is just a hoax. We the people have enough to worry about without that kind of garbage being shoved in our face and demonstrated to our children in school.

Talking about schooling, gee someone has come up with the idea to do away with schools and make home schooling our future. It will be mandatory that each home have a computer so that your child does his schooling by internet. Can you imagine how much more it will cost parents to pay for babysitters? It will be too expensive for any wife/mother to work. What is wrong with the way things are now? A child learns a lot more in life by leaving the home every day and experiencing different things. It is a part of learning. Not everything can be taught over the internet. Children will become withdrawn and not be able to cope with people. This is a bad idea. We must truly hope that this is not going to be a major issue in the future.

Just how many times is the government going to extend unemployment benefits? I realize that it is beneficial for the government to be in control so that we have to rely on them for money, but enough is enough. The government is crippling our society by doling out more and more money to the unemployed. It makes them lazy and dependent. A couple extensions should be enough for people to get back on their feet. Especially if that individual is trying to help themselves. Extra help could be available by giving out some food stamps to help people get back on their feet. It would be cheaper in the long run to help and assist someone out of work, than it would be to give them a paycheck.

There has to be other ways to help individuals then to dole out dollar after dollar while someone sits on their ass and doesn't even try to look for a job. Those jobs that these laid off workers were employed at are still there, at least many of them are. This basically falls under the category of helping one's self.

As for one of the problems that have been a big issue for many is the illegal immigrants. We must quit catering to these individuals. Why do our laws protect the illegals? A fantastic idea would be to arrest all illegals and punish them by making them build a wall between Mexico and us. Their punishment would be hard labor. They would build a wall that would help control this situation. We would not have to spend any money paying to have this done except for supplies and food to feed them, which would be a lot cheaper than us paying laborers to construct this wall. What a better punishment for them to help build the very barrier that they once snuck across into the United States. After a certain amount of time, they then would be dropped off on their side of the wall, and considered time served. We all know why the government tends to protect them and that is based on politics and votes.

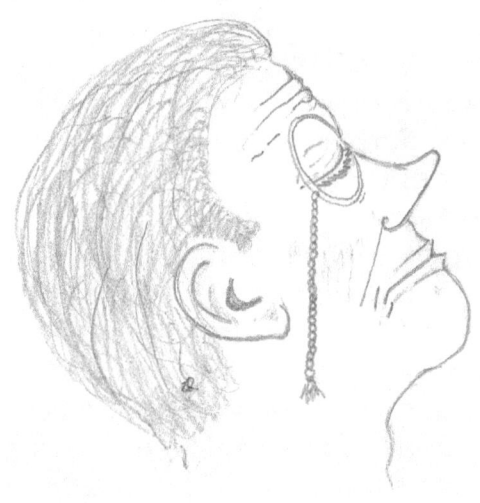

Chapter 6................ Mr. Congeniality

Obama wanting to put a spending freeze on the Whitehouse is a joke. They have already spent the money so it's a little too late to do this. Since they want so much control perhaps they should concentrate on the prices us consumers have to pay for things, such as gasoline, propane, cable, satellite, medical costs, and of course we can go on and on. The problem is that Obama is to busy paying off all the people that helped him get elected. So, now he has no time for such trivial things like helping out the citizens of the United States of America. What is his responsibility as a President? It's obvious that it's not looking out for our best interest. If he were, our Country would be in much better shape than it is now.

The unemployment percentage is higher than it has been in years, many years. It is so easy for Obama to blame the Bush administration. If he spent as much time on the present day problems and less time on what Bush supposedly did, than we would be much better off. It's always easier to blame the other guy in hopes it will make him look better.

When listening to one of Obama's speeches, a person needs a dictionary to decipher every thing he says. This is how we got into this mess. Majority of the population did not understand what he was saying and very little of what he meant. But boy he sure did sound good Heh? We don't need a dictionary for a President. Being President isn't much different than being a parent. In this case a Dad, who should be understanding, lead by example, give guidance, be concerned, teach structure, show fairness, teach the principals of success and failure, encouragement, and how to love and respect others. But our Daddy (Obama) doesn't fill these shoes. He wants to lead with an iron fist, he uses bribery, is power hungry, wants success regardless at what cost, sneaky, conniving, misleads the citizens, lies, and most of all we just can't trust him to be there for us. Because of the company he keeps and the people he chooses to be his Czars we must not allow him to remain in the Whitehouse another term.

The scary part about Obama's feelings is he doesn't care if he serves another term. What message does this send to us? Makes me wonder what is on his agenda. The odds are we don't know and maybe we don't want to know. Why would he not care, unless it will only take these four years to complete his mission?

Which is? Stay tuned for another year of a Progressive Democrat in action, listening to his promises that he does not keep, and watching trillions of dollars just disappear.

Obama is a likeable person, very distinguished, dresses well and carries him self tall and proud. However, this is a Presidential position that he holds. If we were voting on Mr. Congeniality he would probably win. But we are not. What seems to be and what really is happens to be the problem. Although he fits Mr. Congeniality, it is only a front; he has other traits that are hidden and must be of our main concern.

It is really amazing to watch him give the State of the Union speech. As we listen to him, he speaks with such power and assures us that he will resolve our every problem and solve them with dignity and sureness. It's like he makes us feel better about how things are and how strong his intentions are to better our situation. Then weeks later, he has turned every thing around and what we thought he meant wasn't even close. He has a way of tricking his audience and then stabbing us in the back when we let our guard down. The promises that he continues to make are just ploys to get reelected. But my dear fellow Americans we can not let this man back into office. Don't let his quick wits and distinguished manners trick you. He has an agenda and believe me, we as citizens of the United States are a big part of his agenda and us loosing our freedom.

Chapter 7...................... Holiday Spirit

Americans and others around the world all celebrate holidays differently. Each religion and belief has its own traditions. All these traditions were started hundreds of years ago, with each holiday having a special meaning. We as Americans practice these traditions because we grew up believing in them and therefore have become accustomed to that kind of holiday lifestyle.

Now please tell me why a true American would complain about Christmas? Recently I heard from the media that certain states do not want the spirit or the mention of this holiday in their schools. What in the hell is going on? Why would you take this from our children? It is a holiday of sparking lights, rainbows of bright colors, the awaiting moment for Santa in hopes to receive that special gift of love. A joy each and every child remembers through out their whole life. This holiday is a spirit of kindness and love along with giving. It is actually the festival of Christ's nativity. This rumor just blows my mind. Truly people, I just want to beat the daylights out of who ever has come up with this idea. These individuals are not true Americans and should not be listened to.

As a child, the morning of Christmas has stayed in my memories as one of the most exciting times of my life. As I walked down the stairs, I could see a Christmas tree with lights just glowing, as I inched down each step I could see the living room full of color and gifts covered with a snow like substance that sparkled and glittered. The gifts were wrapped with the shiniest paper I had ever seen. The excitement grew bigger as I reached the bottom of the steps, just knowing that Santa brought me that doll I wanted that could walk and say mama. On the other hand I wanted socks and a pretty blouse and of course everything and anything that Santa dropped off was going to be fine in my eyes. We always had to eat breakfast first before we could open our gifts. I ate quickly and ate all my breakfast so as I might get to open my presents quicker.

Ah the time has come and what a delight. Each present had to be shook of this glistening snow and sometimes it would fall on my lap and I would smile with joy. How exciting this moment was. I still remember the days. But now some dumb ass wants to cheat a child out of this joy. It is so hard to believe that someone out here in our America wants to destroy this event. My only hope is that some one puts a stop to this nonsense. This is the land with the spirit of Santa Claus, and we should always be remembered by this holiday of joy. Holidays are very important for people, to bring up ones spirits and have something to look forward to. Life needs these ups that the holidays can fill.

Another holiday of great importance is Thanksgiving Day. Does any one know why it is called Thanksgiving? It was a day established by George Washington as the first national Thanksgiving Day on November 26, 1789 to give thanks to the new Constitution of the United States of America. Now tell me this is not worth celebrating. This fine document has been the structure of our existence and we do owe thanks for this article of direction and the dedication, our founding fathers put into this masterpiece. It is disgusting to know that our President and Congress fail to appreciate and honor the meaning behind this document.

With this being said, it truly is a time to vote out the losers and vote in the people with the commitment and dedication in making our Country proud once again.

Easter is another holiday of great meaning for the Christians. It is a commemoration of the resurrection of Christ. Being a festival it was and is common to dress up and wear cute little bonnets. Through the years the Easter bunny and his eggs have become a part of Easter. What would Easter be like if there were no Easter egg hunts? I can not understand who would want to dismiss these holidays. To each and everyone out in our society, we all find a different way to celebrate each holiday. Some sway toward the more spiritual side and others go for the fantasy side.

Who cares how each one of us celebrates these occasions? What gives some one the right to try to delete them from life, by banning them from our schools? This is not good. Now we have people trying to tell us what to believe in. Please don't let this happen. For the individuals that are against these holidays, then get the hell out of our Country.

I almost have to laugh when I think of the saying America the Land of the Free. Not anymore. The good thing about it is that there are still millions of people who will not give up their freedom with out a fight.

They always say there are two things you do not discuss, one being politics and the other being religion. However, these two subjects bring up some huge debates that can be taken out of text. You either believe in God or you don't. There is the theory of evolution that many sway toward. There is truly no proof of either so what harm is there in believing the way we want to? As with politics there is the good the bad and the ugly. Just what do you believe in? We should not be judged on our beliefs, but on how we treat our peers. Honesty is still the best policy. It will take you down the path of the least destruction and gain respect of everyone you encounter.

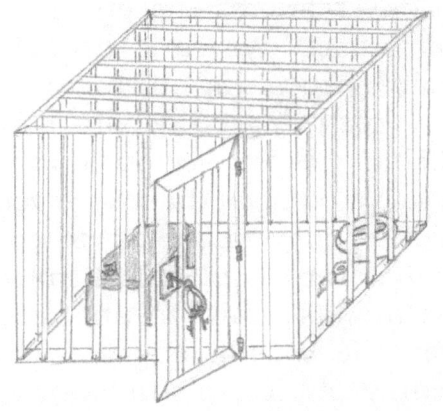

Chapter 8.................................Freedom

The true meaning of freedom is the state of being free, frankness and the facility of doing anything. We all know what it's like to be free. At this point in time our freedom is in jeopardy. The days of saying and doing what we want are coming to an end.

The first amendment of the Constitution states that the government can not prohibit our freedom of speech, or that of the press. It also states we have the right to assemble to petition the government regarding any grievances. The Obama administration is still continuing to go against our Constitution.

How will we tolerate being controlled by our government? Just recently a town in California arrested someone because of political and religious conversations.

How disgusting this is to think that we can no longer express our opinions about anything with out fear of going to jail. Conversation between individuals is very important to our society. We learn through conversation. We communicate by speaking our minds. It is good to be opinionated and open. A good debate is always good for the soul. Not being able to voice our opinions will create problems. Why is it so crucial that our government control our conversations? They might try to control what we say, but they will never be able to control what we think. Being an American has always meant freedom of speech. This is no longer true. We still must ask why? What is our Whitehouse scared of? It looks like our rights are here today and gone tomorrow.

If our opinions are going to be attacked, than the press will have a problem reporting the news. That is probably the reason our conversations are being policed, because they don't want us to know the real news. The less we as Americans know then the more the government can get away with. They are getting sneakier every day and we better start watching them before all our rights are gone.

The government makes many bad comments about Fox News and that leads me to believe that Fox News is telling us like it is and they don't like it. Before long I would not be surprised if they banned Fox News from discussing any government issues. When and if that time comes we all better pack up and leave the Country.

I never thought I would see the day when I could not speak freely and say what's on my mind. Being a very opinionated person, along with many out there, that are, it will be a struggle to get along and hold back our thoughts. This would put many of us in a world of trouble. This is a right that no one wants to loose. This must not happen to us as Americans. We must stand our ground and never let this be a threat to us. So far we still have the right to vote and now it's time to clean house. I say, out with the jerks that are trying to take our rights away.

The Second Amendment states that the people have the right to bear arms. Meaning we the people may have guns. The government is against us having guns. They have mentioned that they are considering banning firearms in the United States. We must not let that happen. We need our guns. My guess is that if we are armed and can defend ourselves, then the government could not gain the control that they want over us. Back many years ago there would not be dinner on the table if it were not for a gun. They had to hunt for their meals. They skinned and cleaned and cooked their catch and then sat down and ate dinner. If times were to get bad again and you couldn't go to the super market and buy meat, then we would have to resort back to killing it ourselves and preparing it. If our guns are taken away and times get hard, we could all starve to death. Our weapons are important and have many uses. A gun can provide food, protect you from a wild animal, protect you from a psychopath and be your best friend in case of war.

This is our right and no one should be able to take our guns away. For those of you who don't like guns then don't own one. Don't go around anyone that may have a gun. That is your right. But don't step on my toes just because you don't like guns, it's only fair. Yes there are people, who abuse this right, but those people are criminals and we all know what happens to them. If we abuse anything it can cause consequences. We the people need to protect our rights, especially the right to bear arms. It's mandatory for our existence.

Another thing that bothers me is why the government tries to control our habits.

Such as smoking... If a person wants to smoke then that should be up to them. We all know it isn't good for us, but that is what some of us choose to do. It's a better habit than drinking, but nothing is ever said about booze. Alcohol causes many health problems. Not only health problems but a drunk is very annoying. They smell bad, they talk terrible, and they stagger, not to mention some people actually get mean on alcohol. But yet it's okay to drink as long as you don't get caught drinking and driving. If anything should be banned from society, it should be alcohol. A cigarette doesn't cause accidents. It still has not been determined that even the second hand smoke is bad. So I guess it's better to be an alcoholic than a smoker huh? A better idea would be for the government to mind their own damn business.

We do need the government for many things, but telling us how to live our lives is not one of them. Do you know how many Senators and Governors have bad habits such as drinking and smoking? It is hard to believe that they can get any bill passed considering how many of them smoke or drink, especially drink. Gee it's just not tobacco or alcohol, but they disobey many other laws. How many times have you heard about this problem? Even our President's are guilty of this. They make it sound like we the people are the criminals. Yet we couldn't compare to the Whitehouse's reputation.

Perhaps they should clean out their own backyards before they start on ours. Our rights are more important to us than you may realize. Becoming an American is another situation that Congress fails to adhere to. What about the immigrants? This is America and if you want to be an American you need to speak English and go through the proper channels to do so. We are too easy on the immigrants, and it's high time that we tighten our shoe strings and demand that becoming a citizen is mandatory in order to be accepted as an American. This includes their health care or any other kind of care that our Country offers.

It appears that the government has more rights than we do. Is this right? They work for us. We vote them in to office under the pretense that they are going to support us and go to battle for us. But no, they take away our rights and pretend that they are on our side. Then they push through bills that we are against and force feed us policies that we do not approve of. It makes me sick to be lied to by the very people that we trusted and put into office. Something has to be done by us very soon. Obama made many promises and yet all he does is put us further in debt.

We will never have freedom again thanks to Obama. The Bush administration did have us in debt but there was light at the end of the tunnel. Now Obama has put us in a situation that darkens our Country and we have become a slave to our Nation because of owing all this money. Thanks Obama for everything. Now it's time for you to step down and let someone else step up to secure our Nation and help make our Country free again. You will definitely go down in history, but it won't be for every thing you have done for us, but everything you have destroyed during your journey as a President. You are trying to infringe upon our rights. I am going to exercise my right to free speech and say Please get out of office and resign, you are no longer needed, wanted or liked. The majority rules, you know, you have played the game.

"If Nancy Pelosi and Obama were in a boat out in the middle of the ocean, and it started to sink, do you know who would be saved? America."

When we speak of freedom, there is a sigh of relief just hearing that word. We must think about the 13 year old boy who rode his bicycle to school every day with an American flag attached to his bike. Just why did this young teen get into trouble for being patriotic and have to take the flag off his bike? The school decided that he had to take it off. That doesn't say much for our school system. It is hard enough to get a teenager interested in patriotism let alone getting them to understand what being a true American is. Here is a young man proud to be an American and displaying it on his bicycle and he has to remove it. I would like to know what jerk decided to make him remove it. This is just another fine example of what our Country is becoming. I guess the un-Americans that attend school were offended by it. This is to damn bad.

This is America and we have the right to be proud and display our flag. If the foreigners in our Country are offended by our flag, than get the hell out of America. We must refuse to appease the foreigners who have come to our Nation and try to change us and our beliefs. This is the only free Country left. If our freedom dwindles down to zilch, then the world will be run by money hungry politicians and we will be their slaves.

Our government continues to move swiftly in making sure they have all the control. By them being control freaks, it lessens our knowledge of what's going on. They want to deprive us of knowledge. It is to their advantage. The less we know, the easier it becomes for them to be malicious. They even do it right in front of our faces and we are not aware of what is going on.

Chapter 9............................Decisions

M aking decisions is one of the most important things
a President has to do. The problem with Obama is
that he makes poor decisions.

Drilling for oil, for example is a major dilemma for the
United States. But what many of us wonder is, Why don't
we drill for oil in our Country? The foreign Countries are
raping us on oil prices. It would seem we could cut cost
and be less dependent on these other Countries if we just
drill for our own oil. We have the capability and the oil
source, so someone please give us a logical explanation
of why we are still buying oil from another Country.

There are trillions of barrels of oil here in the United
States, especially in North and South Dakota. What
about Alaska, we can drill on the outer shelf of the shore
line and produce about 10 billion barrels of oil, which in

return would create about 55,000 jobs. So, why are we in the shape were in? We actually have more oil than Saudi Arabia and all the other Countries. It does not make sense, but does bring up a red flag as to what is going on? It looks like Obama is doing this on purpose, to weaken us and keep us as the under dog. We need to be more independent when it comes to our fuel sources. Its bad enough we owe our Country to China for trillions of dollars. The United States has never had to count on other Countries like we do now. I don't like it. It makes us a weak Nation.

Obama speaks about bettering our exports, and having more Countries rely on us. What can we possibly make to export? The unions have taken over so bad that we can no longer afford to manufacture anything for minimal monies. China can produce thousands of items made very cheaply allowing them to make a profit. Our costs would be so high for manufacturing that there would be no profits.

What have we done to ourselves? We have out priced our own goods leaving no room for profits, putting us in the position of having to rely on another Country. Before we can strengthen our exports we must destroy the unions. That will never happen because of the millions of dollars they gave to Obama for his campaign.

Obama talks about creating all these jobs. Please tell us what jobs were created? In my eyes the only way to create jobs is to open business's that can employ many people. A great idea would be a government store stocked similar to the items in a Wal-Mart store. A huge department type store that sells things at a reasonable cost. They could be opened in each state. With the economy being iffy, it would help the unemployed. There are many other kinds of business's that could be opened. After all it would be more profitable for the government to invest in opening some stores as opposed to the way they are blowing our money now.

These stores could also work by employing the laid off workers so that the government would not have to pay unemployment wages, therefore saving more of our money. Each unemployed person would work for a wage that would equal their unemployment compensation, until they were able to get another job. It would help the economy and the government would still profit from the sale of items.

A new law should be enforced to stop mortgage payments for someone who has a mortgage and can not find a job. The bank or finance company where a person's loan is, would agree to this ruling, allowing people not to loose their homes right away. Of course there would be a time period that this would be good for, so as not to allow someone to take advantage of the system. I really feel better decisions should be made in regards to our Countries unemployment rate.

Poor decisions are affecting our Country, especially when it comes to this war. Our soldiers are risking their lives to protect us and I think that we should be making good decisions to protect our soldiers. No soldier wants to be in another Country fighting and risking their life with out some meaning or a mission that will be accomplished quickly and proudly. When Obama is asked for more troops I think he should immediately oblige. But he hesitated and did not agree to the amount of soldiers needed for the mission. I say lets go over there and show them whose boss. Blow them all to hell and bring back our soldiers. The reason for us being there is pretty understandable when it comes to dealing with these Terrorists. However, let's get the job done and come home. Why are we dragging our feet, loosing soldiers and wasting money on this war?

Another decision that I think will be bad for all of us is this Cap and Trade bill. It will raise our utility bills so high that none of us will be able to afford them. It's so hard right now to pay some of our heating bills, just how will we be able to make it if the cost soars higher?

Soon they will be enforcing energy efficient home standards. You will need a license posted in your home whether it is energy friendly or not. We will all suffer from the cost of up grading our homes to the new government standards. If it does not meet their guide lines you will never be able to sell your home. Because of this, many people will loose their homes because they will not be able to afford the upgrades that their homes will need. This is a terrible thing to do to us when the economy is so bad and many people are out of work. We do not need any more government forced rules that cost us an arm and a leg. Our homes have been just fine through out the years with the way things are now. With the government owning 95% of home mortgages it will be easy for them to make any new rulings on the upgrade of our homes. As it is now, house sales are declining and the property values are going down.

We must object to this Cap and Trade bill and let it be known that we will not tolerate this. I don't think it will matter to them but we must try to stop it. There are so many ways to look at global warming. After watching Al Gore's video on global warming, it sure did scare me and many into thinking this really was going to happen. Others believe that global warming is just a hoax and mostly to scare us. Let's face it we can not control Mother Nature. She will perform as she sees fit and we have to live with it. But in the mean time why does Congress want us to pay out our, you know what? These decisions are not healthy for Americans. It will cause more delinquent bills and the low income individuals will struggle even harder. Our government is going to put us in a bind and we can not allow this to happen to us. We must put our foot down and fight this bill to the end. Those people working in the Whitehouse make a whole lot more money than we do and it would not be detrimental to their finances like it would be ours.

We must all take time to think through these new bills and laws that the government wants to enforce.

We should all be concerned about the out come of this. Saving food and water and survival items would be a good idea if we want to make it through the next century.

What do you think of the big Oil spill? Was it really an accident? Perhaps, but isn't it kind of strange that now the oil wells have to be capped and no more drilling is allowed, But we are paying for the drilling of oil elsewhere and Obama and others have invested in this and now will make a fortune. This all sounds a little fishy to me. We must take note of the moves that are being taken by our government, because they are only doing things that will put money in their pockets and put America at risk.

It is kind of weird that Obama's dad was a Communist and had some vicious dreams to do harm to America and now Obama wants to see to it that he fulfills his dad's dreams. America, we did not do our homework. We have allowed an evil man to rule our Nation and we are going to pay for our mistakes. When will Congress wake up and see the light.

My fear is that many of our government officials are just as sneaky and evil as our President and it has just taken years to accomplish the situation that is now a present threat to us Americans. The decision to raise taxes is going to be so hard on us Americans. If we truly had good representation in office, we would not be drowning in debt.

When it comes to decision making, who do you think came up with the Transportation Security Administration? This is basically enforcing security at our airports. But the choice they made to do this is upsetting millions of people. How do you feel about the new body X-ray machines now at the airports? Or better yet, if you don't want to go through this machine that's okay because you can choose to get patted down. In other words, frisked or felt up. Gee what a choice we have. We can either choose radiation treatments or have someone fondle your breast or grab at your crotch. These choices are unacceptable to our society. Yes we want to secure our planes from Terrorists, but isn't there another way? Other Countries have airport security and they aren't zapping people with radiation or fondling parts of an individual's body. There truly has to be another way that is cheaper and more acceptable. With all the modern day technology and smart scientists, one would think that something else could be done.

Sometimes I wonder if there isn't a method behind the government's madness. Actually we shouldn't wonder if there is, there has to be. But because we are kept in the dark we will probably never know the real secrets behind the enemy line, being our government.

A poor decision was made when someone came up with the idea to use our food crops for fuel. This is not good. It requires a lot of corn to be able to heat your house. Which lessens our food source from corn? Corn is used in many things we eat. It doesn't help matters when the government pays farmers not to grow crops. How is it beneficial to pay someone not to grow something? It's bad enough food prices are at a record high, they will continue to go higher yet. Perhaps people will understand a little better when they can't afford to buy a can of corn.

As we all know, we are basically going into war with Libya. This is a little shady if I say so myself. This will be three wars that we are involved in. Can we really afford this? No of course not. But when you have all the money that Obama does then I guess we can. But the big decision maker Obama has decided that we will battle it out over there but we are going to leave our soldiers there and be under the command of someone else. Not us, like it should be, but a committee called the Political Steering Committee with a Canadian General being in charge. Who the hell decided that? Our soldiers are risking their lives at the command of a stupid committee. Something is not right here. Just maybe Obama doesn't want to be involved because of the Muslim's. Do you suppose this could be right?

Since when does our military go into battle under the command of strangers from other Countries? After all, who are we fighting on behalf of? Well American's, we have heard it all now.

We have got the Islamic terrorist's and the leftist wanting to change our Western Way of Life and now we are casually giving America up to a committee. We are fighting in three different Countries with the majority of individuals being Muslim's and we're just going to walk away and let someone tell our soldiers what to do. This is not right, not good, and not ethical and it's just ridiculous.

Chapter 10 ....Tea Party Movement

What a pleasant name for a group of people who are concerned with the choices our government is making. Majority of us should be involved in the Tea Party Movement. Obviously we want the government to hear us and stop all this nonsense. But they will not stop. They will continue to rub us the wrong way and interfere with our life and our money.

I for one would love to be involved in each and everyone of these rallies. But many of us can not afford to take time off from work and in some cases we can not afford the plane tickets to get to the state in which they are at. If you think about it these Tea Parties are really great ways to show the government that we are not happy with them and we do not agree with what they have in store for us.

It is nice to know that the people involved in these Tea Parties are very calm collective individuals. There is no mob like violence or disturbing threats to anyone. All these people want is to be heard and are hoping that the government is listening and thinking about what we the people want. It is kind of strange that the media does not report more on them than we hear about. But I think Obama tries to control the media to the point where we only can hear what he wants us to. Isn't this sickening? Perhaps the Presidents have a little bit too much power and we should consider controlling the power they have. The strangest part about it all is, they act like we don't exist, and like we have no objections and basically we're not even there.

These Tea Parties are pep rallies for the Americans who want to voice their opinions and complain about how we are being treated and ignored. They consist of Democrats, Republicans and Independents. Majority are Conservatives. All they really want is to be heard. Just being heard is not enough, we want results. We want these bills that are going to cost us trillions of dollars to be denied. We voted you into office people so please honor our wishes and vote these bad boys down.

It appears that our Senators and House members are afraid of Obama, if they weren't why would they vote yes on these bills? It would have to affect them also; after all they do live in the same world as us, Right? Even if they are bribed, you would think that they would not want to have to pay all these added expenses either.

My dear fellow Americans let's do all we can to be heard and let the government know that we are not happy with their decisions or the bills that come across the table. Not only will we suffer but our children as well. Socialism/Communism is closer than you think.

What is it going to take? We have Tea Parties gathering together to show our concerns with the governments decisions. We have been included in many polls that give a percentage on how we feel. Yet, the Whitehouse keeps on truckin. They ignore us to the point of desperation and concern. We want our rights back.

If we want to eat 5 candy bars, and smoke 3 packs a day then that's our damn business and not theirs. If we don't want to have government health care then don't make us. If we want our thermostats on 80, then so be it. Why is it that our right to exist and our freedom are being tampered with? We as Americans know there are consequences if you disobey the law. But now the laws are getting to trivial. Our lawmakers are pushing our buttons and we should fear the end result.

It is so nice to see thousands of Americans gather together to send a message to Congress that we are not happy. But can you believe the audacity of Nancy Pelosi? This brazen smug individual walked through the Tea Party with a gavel as big as can be, just to rub it into our faces when the Health Care Bill was passed. What kind of person would do such a thing to us, we the people who have conveyed by many means that we do not want a Health Care Bill? She just did this to start trouble so her and her sidekicks could say that the Tea Party was a violent group. But we held our composure and held our heads up high as she strutted through the crowd. Good thing she could not read our minds. I am sure she would have fell to the ground and screamed for help, if she only knew what we all thought of her and her actions. At that time, she was actually trying to cause trouble.

Next time she wants to prance through a crowd, I hope it's the crowd that watches her as she leaves office permanently.

Do you find it strange that Stupak decided to resign? The Tea Party was right on his ass and knew he was a traitor. Stupak stated that he had been trying to get a Health Care Program for eighteen years and decided it was time to retire. I think he was concerned with how much pressure was coming his way because of his voting.

We all have Fox News to be thankful for. They tell it like it is. Just think how dumb founded we would be if it weren't for Fox News. It is important to all of us Americans to know what is going on and who is behind it all. It is scary to think that the other news channels do not tell the whole story behind things. They say "What you don't know won't hurt you." But when it comes to Congress and Obama, we better hope we know everything because what we don't know is definitely going to hurt us. Look how much we do know and it is all bad news and probably will hurt us in the long run.

My dear fellow Americans we must be alert more than ever in our lives. We must listen and make good decisions. Don't ever think that America can not fail or go under. Because it can happen and it will happen if we let Obama and Congress do what they have planned for us. The only way we have to fight back is our right to vote. So please, I beg every one to vote out the Socialists and Communist, so that America can be free once again.

People did not know that Obama was a Socialist, because he kept it hidden. When he is confronted with this comment, the only thing he has to say is, we have no proof. But he did not deny it and that is the strange part of it all. I would say that the proof is in his comment; he just says we have no proof. Well the proof we have is in his actions and his decision making. We can see how he tricked us, so now it is so important to study the back ground of any person running for office.

As it turns out Sarah Palin has backed many Conservatives running for office. The great thing about this is that over 75% of the individuals she backed actually got voted into office in 2010. This is remarkable. Maybe she should play the ponies; it seems she can pick out the good guys, at least so far. She has traveled to many places to speak to us Americans to broaden our mind and help us with some decision making of our own.

She is number one in my book. She just has a smile that makes you feel welcomed and a personality that makes you want to stick around and hear what else she has to say. I can see why the Tea Party likes her to speak. What a great backer.

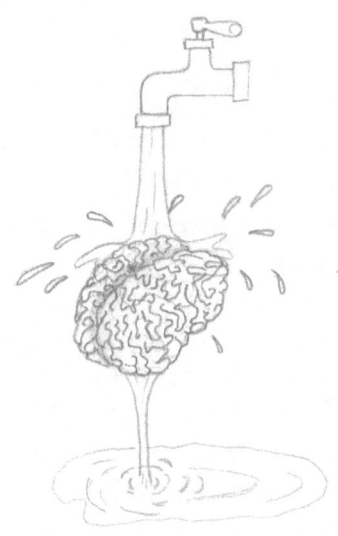

Chapter 11 ....Brainwashing

Have you seen how the children are being brainwashed in the schools? They are singing songs about Obama and being taught that Socialism is good. They are being introduced to Radical behaviors of leaders that are known to be very bad people in history. Do you want your children learning this? They are trying to destroy our children's prior beliefs. They are conditioning our kids to behave and believe differently than what we have taught them. How far will they go? These people want control over us, but because it's a little harder to brainwash us adults, they are going after our kids. There young and easy to persuade in a direction that we all should fear. This is unacceptable and must be stopped.

Please parents, pay attention to what your kids are being taught and how they react to each other during play time. Are they more aggressive than usual? Are they trying to be to bossy to their friends? Has their compassion begun to dissolve? Have they begun to talk back to you as an outsider instead of a parent? These all could be signs that your child believes more in what he is fed in school than the normal morals that a child should have. The children are being taught that they are much smarter than their parents. It is a shame that they are turning the children against the parents by demeaning their intelligence. It isn't right for someone to lead your kids to believe that parents are stupid and don't know as much as the kids. This causes problems with parental control. This is just another trick on our lawmaker's part to brainwash our children into believing their ways and not what the parents are teaching them.

Weak minds are easy to brainwash. These tricks were done years ago when Hitler was in charge. Brainwashing is the first step in controlling the people. Once we believe in their ideas than we must obey them and be told when, what, where and how to live. America must not fall under the hand of this kind of society. We are strong individuals with sound minds and we must remain strong to conquer the intrusion of these evil people. Is it possible that Obama is behind this kind of society? Many people must be willing to work together to try to take away our freedom. We need to sort them out and destroy their plans. It all sounds a little paranoid but is it? Things are beginning to pop up that just are not normal for a Country like ours.

Remember hearing about Reverend Wright, Obama's friend, and was the Reverend of the church he went to for twenty years? In one clip on TV you saw him cursing America and saying "Damn America". After Obama heard that for all those years, you mean to tell me that it didn't sink into his head. How can you not wonder if he has been brainwashed for years and years. Now he comes forward and leads our Country, and puts us all in debt to the point of no recovery. Our Nation is being damned alright, it's being destroyed by a man of ill teachings, an arrogant individual who was taught to seek out and destroy America as quickly as possible and put the hurt on our Nation's functions. Makes you wonder Huh?

In order to take over our Nation, a plan that has been in effect for many years is now starting to show. Look at our children. The government is protecting them in a strange way. They are making them meek and weak. After all when these children grow up to be adults they will have been weaned on a society based on every thing being given to them on a silver platter. They will not be strong willed, they will have no back bone or stamina. That's exactly what the government wants. It will be much easier for them to take control of them and push them around and do more brainwashing on them.

Look how times have changed; remember when the back windows in the cars rolled down all the way? Not any more, they are only allowed to roll down half way. This is ridiculous. As kids we never fell out of the back window or had a desire to jump out of a moving car. So why the big change? Why turn our children into pansies?

What about the issue on using a red ink pen to grade their school work? Come on, this is so petty. This is supposed to be upsetting to a child to see the red ink. I remember when I was a kid it didn't matter what color it was, it was important that the grade was passing and not failing. Who the hell thought this one up?

All through school it was always normal to aim to do better, but now kids get participation trophies. This is not rewarding, this is saying to a child that they do not have to try to better themselves because they will still get an award any way. What is going on in our society? Why are we making the children weaker and less responsible for their actions and their decisions? Our children will not know what it's like to have to try their best and to do better and to exceed the next person. That is life, which is how we build character, establish our personality and train ourselves for future endeavors. By making those weak and unable to fend for themselves will create a new kind of society, one that is easy for the government to control. All trophies and awards should be earned and deserved, not just handed out for being involved.

We should be very bothered by the new laws and new systems that are created in raising our children. What ever happened to Corporate Punishment? It was good for the kids to know that if they were bad they got a ruler over the knuckles or had to stand in the corner or even get a swat on the butt in front of the whole school? In those times kids behaved better and had more respect for others. Now days they are foolish and run rampart as they get out of control. It is no wonder the schools are having trouble with the students.

The schools have lost control of the kids, and because of this, it will be hard to enforce any discipline. Society will pay for this. We may not see it in our lifetime, but it is just around the corner. Children need discipline, punishment and guidance. Without those, this world will go to hell. Or, the government will push the parents aside as they brainwash the children and teach them that they are smarter than their parents. Problems will arise out of this kind of system. There will be chaos and before you know it, all parents will loose control of their children as the government gains control. We do not want this to happen.

Many states are going to a 4 day school week to cut cost. I see other problems arising from this situation. What are these kids suppose to do with an extra day off school? It is going to create boredom which in return will cause them to get in to more trouble. Their parents are going to have to pay out more money trying to find a babysitter for that extra day off. We all know that the teachers are not going to take a cut in pay, so how are they really cutting cost? Our children do not need more time on their hands, especially when both parents now days have to work to make a go of it. The less supervision a child receives will create more havoc in the future.

Because the adults in America are strong willed and have grown up with their beliefs from their childhood, it makes it harder for the government to control us. But by making our children weak and unaccountable for their actions, it will help the government in the future to take better control of the population. So our children are the real targets in this millennium of change, redistribution and Socialism tactics. Children are easily manipulated and an easy target to persuade and guide in a direction, that we as adults do not want any part of. We can not allow our government to get to our children.

Now the government has taken control of all student loans. You see, they are still working on the younger generation to take control of them. By Obama taking over the schools and college's it will fall right into his plan to manipulate our Country. This back door Socialism that is involved in the student loan situation is not good. It's just a matter of time before they start choosing our children's careers. And soon Obama will have to approve which college they can attend.

The cost of education will go through the roof and we can not afford more taxes. By them offering more grants, will cost us taxpayers more money. After all, someone has to pay for those grants. There are so many problems with public education, because we have taken control from the teachers and the schools. The children have too many choices and have it too good. They are more concerned about texting their friends as opposed to doing their work assignment. Kids learn much better and become more involved in school functions when they don't have distractions like cell phones, blackberries and I-pods.

Modern day technology has made it harder for kids to pay attention in school. Children don't need all the frills out there, they need education and morals. Right now, I think both of those are slipping away.

Those of you with children will soon be in for a big surprise, because in a school in New York the children are not allowed to bring their own lunch to school. Do you realize that parents will now be expected to pay for their child to eat lunch at school? This is just another demand and control situation that we need to highly object to. If lunch is $2.00 a day times 5 days, it will cost each parent $40.00 a month just for their child's lunch. Not only will you pay for their lunch but they are taking away the choice of having chocolate milk. This is ridiculous, as you will see. This has to do with parent's not being capable of feeding their children properly. I'm sure your slowly getting the picture of what is about to take place in our Country.

My dear fellow Americans, marinate on this for awhile because the government will continue to take over step by step, inch by inch until we abide by all their new laws, and then before we know it, we are victims in our own society. It's just a matter of time.

Chapter 12............................. Congress

In article I of the Constitution, section 9, paragraph 7, it states that a regular statement and account of the receipts and expenditures of all public money be published from time to time.

Congress does not allow us to see these expenses. They should be posted periodically so that we citizens can see what they are spending our money on. We have no idea where and what our money is being spent on. What if we don't approve of this? I am amazed that Congress can get away with this. We all want to know where the money is going. And why is it taking billions of dollars now to make our payments and yet in the past we did not have to keep borrowing like we are now?

Our Senator's and Governor's who live in different states are using our money for transportation back and forth to the Whitehouse. This is upsetting. All members of Congress should be paying for this out of their pockets, not ours. If they can not afford to do so, then they should move closer to the Whitehouse. After all, we all have to pay our transportation to and from work and so should they. Here is some more of our taxpayer's dollars going to waste. Who the hell do they think they are? This makes us sick to see them use our taxes inappropriately. This is one expense that we could cut down on. There are so many things that Congress spends money on that is not necessary but convenient for them.

It's time for us Americans to tighten their spending. Someone must get into our Congress and stop this wasteful spending. Perhaps if we all quit paying taxes, they would really feel what it's like to be broke. Who paid for Mr. & Mrs. Obama and Oprah Winfrey's flight when they went to Copenhagen to see about getting the Olympics to come to Illinois? We did. Actually we paid for two trips. How much do you think that cost? Well let's see, they took their relatives, and the motel cost $4000.00 a night, then there were food expenses for everyone. Gee almost a million dollar trip. I bet that would have paid many Social Security checks for our senior citizens or might have even lowered our debt, but no, just another wasteful adventure. Now I am wondering who pays for all Obama's golfing and outings. Not to mention what Michelle Obama blows money on that we tax payers are paying for.

How about the money Obama wants to spend on studying college football? Do you think that's coming out of his pocket? You got it.... How about the study on how many beers a person drinks or how much marijuana they smoke? Is this study so important that we need to spend thousands of dollars researching it? This is not a good time to waste money when we are so far in debt.

This Stimulus money is just another bank account for Obama and his sidekicks to use for whatever. There is enough money there for everyone in the United States to pay off every bill they have and become debt free, and still have enough to run our Nation. It sounds like we have some greedy bastards running our Country.

My advice to Congress would be, look out, because the American people are catching on to your evil ways. Hopefully this book I have written will turn on a light bulb in the minds of those who think; nothing will happen and we're above a major break down of our Nation and our existence as we know it.

A true American doesn't want a free ride in life. Basically, we all want to be left alone and live our life. Were not asking for hand outs like government officials receive. Did you happen to notice a TV clip showing a lady jump for joy when Obama won the election because now she would not have to make her house payment any longer? Could you imagine assuming that? There are people that believe that someone out there will help them because they won't help themselves. A news flash for those of you thinking like this.. Shame on you, help only comes to people who try to help themselves. This Country does not need losers, or dictators.

A dictator rules with power and if that does not work they resort to force. Speaking of force, Pelosi sounds like a dictator. As she discussed the Health Care Program that we don't want, she stated if the fence was too high they would climb over it, if that didn't work they would pole-vault over it and if that didn't work they would parachute in, but one way or another they are going to pass this Health Care bill. This woman really needs an attitude adjustment; she is another person we must concentrate on removing from office. Wake up California, can't you see what kind of person she is, not to mention her evil ways. It is nice to know that she got demoted from her position.

She too is guilty of spending too much of our tax payer dollars. Who does she think she is? She and Obama make a good team, almost like Bonnie & Clyde. Their going to steal all the money they can from us and then spend it on wasteful things. With out our tax dollars this Nation could not function. So why aren't our government officials a little thriftier? Maybe in the next few years they too can join the ranks of the unemployed. It would really put a smile on many faces. The more honest our politicians are, the better our Nation will be. However, the search for honest politicians may be a problem but they are out there.

Another huge problem within our government is printing money. Guess what? The money still keeps coming off the press. Now this creates a bigger problem because that makes our money worthless. So a dollar will not be worth a dollar anymore, maybe it will be worth sixty five cents. As the money keeps printing, the amount of our dollar goes down. This means the price of everything will have to go up because it will cost more to buy something. If you spend a dollar on a candy bar now, soon that same candy bar will be $4.75. Now can we afford this? The prices of every thing would not have to soar if the government quit spending money and then printing more money to spend.

It's a vicious cycle and who knows when it will stop. We the people must put an end to government spending.

None of us want China to control our Nation, but soon it could happen. What a disaster that will be. Soon your $10.00 an hour job will become a $2.00 an hour job. But the price of things will still remain the same. Then as in China, every one will be a slave to their Nation. What will happen to our rights, our freedom and liberty for all, well we can **Kiss Freedom Goodbye**?

Another fine idea of Obama's was the Cash for Clunkers Program. Did you know they only sold 125,000 cars during this program? The government sure did waste a lot of money, time and some good vehicles were trashed. How do they sleep at night, when they demanded that the cars that were used for trade-in were crushed? What a waste. Many people could use transportation and can't afford it. But Obama wants to destroy these vehicles. I tell you that was the dumbest, stupidest idea that's ever been done.

Did you know there is a government grant that comes out of our tax money that covers the study of sipping and tasting coffee? Wow. What a waste of money. There are many grants out there that need to be ended before we go broke. How about the study of ants? We dish out money for this also. It's a crying shame that America is so far in debt because of all these studies and grants.

The natural disaster that hit Haiti was terrible and none of us would want to be in their shoes. But did you know that we have been sending Haiti money for years? Why are we doing this? They don't use the money to better their Country, so where is it going? You can probably count on America sending Haiti more money because of their misfortune. We can no longer support these other Nations because we can't take care of our own. It doesn't take a rocket scientist to figure out that it's time to stop this ridiculous spending and taking care of other Nations. We must come first if we want to remain independent.

Tomorrow when you're driving to work, think about where your taxes are going. You won't be too happy to hear this, but the eastern side of the United States is of course on the ocean. We all know that to have a home on the ocean that you are making boo coo dollars. Well, every year the government pays millions of our tax dollars for rebuilding the barricades between the ocean and the person's home that is living there, due to it being washed away. Now then, don't you think that the person owning that home should be responsible for their own damn back yard? If living on the ocean is that much of a hassle and an expense, then perhaps they better move away. It's not fair that we are paying all this money for these people to enjoy their yard on the ocean and we can't even get a pothole filled on the streets we live on. This is another expense that needs looking in to.

You can bet there is millions of dollars going out for things that we don't even know about. If we did, we would just loose it. There was a time that I think we all looked up to the government and considered them our leaders and our mentors. But now their true colors are showing and I for one am disgusted with their decisions on how they spend our money and their sneakiness. The only thing we can learn from them is how crooked and stupid they really are. They are not responsible individuals, just a threat to mankind.

I think it's obvious that there is blackmailing and bribes going on in our political system, why else is our money being spent so foolishly? This money would not be spent so foolishly if pork spending was done away with. Congress gets a bill that is very important and someone throws in another expense they want covered. Because they want the true bill to pass, they automatically approve the foolish one because it was written within it. The only way to stop this pork spending is to read the bills and vote against it until it is written properly and covers the subject in mind and not a bunch of other garbage. Why is this so hard to do?

If we can understand this, then why does Congress allow it to happen? The truth of the matter is, you scratch my back and I'll scratch your back. Actually saying, if you want my vote on this bill, you'll have to pass the other items that are within the bill or I won't vote the way Congress wants me to. And these are the kind of people we have running our society. What bothers me the most is; just how stupid do the politicians think we are? They act like we can't think on our own and that we will believe anything we are told. It's time we let them know just how smart we are, by voting their dumb ass out of there.

The following joke really fits congress; a man walks into a Café with a shotgun in one hand and pulling a male cow in the other hand. He says to the waiter "Coffee Please". The waiter says sure guy coming right up. He gets him a tall mug of coffee. The guy drinks the coffee down in one gulp, turns and blasts the cow with his shotgun, causing parts of the animal to splatter everywhere. And then walks out.

The next morning the guy returns. He has his shotgun in one hand, pulling a male cow with the other. He walks up to the counter and says to the waiter "Coffee Please", the waiter says whoa guy. We're still cleaning up your mess from yesterday. What was that all about? The guy smiles and proudly says "I am in training for a position in the United States Congress; come in, drink coffee, shoot the bull, leave a mess for others to clean up and disappear for the rest of the day."

That definitely describes Congress in a nut shell. It has to be true or why else would we be in this mess? If they were doing their jobs, that they were elected to do, perhaps our Country would be better off.

Almost 86% of the population thinks that the United States is now broken. It would appear that majority of the people would prefer to abolish the government and start over.

Amongst the many bills that Congress does pass, 12 of those bills had 9,500 earmarks in them. What? Costing us about 15.9 billion dollars. This is pitiful. Obama says he would not allow any more earmarks, pork spending. Yet billions of dollars in pork are being wasted. We need to nick name Obama Porky. He is the worst one of them all to allow this kind of ridiculous spending. But I guess we don't have to worry about the earmarks and pork spending any more because they changed the name to Specific Projects. That's really going to help all that wasteful spending just by changing the name. This is so funny, their hoping if they change the name over and over again we will loose track of what their talking about. We are not the idiots here, Congress is.

Obama's lies are actually starting to be funny. Every time he speaks he contradicts the last speech or interview he did. As he speaks the lies just roll off his tongue. I really wonder if he knows that he is lying so much. How could anyone lie that many times and not catch it, himself? What about his relationship with Acorn. First he barely knew them, and then he says he always backs them up. What is his problem?

One thing we all pretty much know is that you just can not trust a liar. They are not reliable people. Their story changes with the weather. How can we put our faith and our trust in a man who continues to lie as he tries to rule our world? We do not need a leader like this. He tricked us all, with his arrogant ways that look distinctive but deceitful. He has the ability to talk circles around some of the best speakers out there, and smile as he stabs us in the back.

Gee, don't you wish we could just get a refund and replace him so we can go on with our lives without worrying about government issues? There was a time that politics was for politicians. Who cared about who wanted what chair or what State Representative was running for office? Now it is detrimental to our well being to ignore any political issue, in fear of it turning our lives upside down.

"One thing about Obama is that everything he says can be fully substantiated by his own opinion."

"A recession is when your neighbors loose their jobs.

A depression is when you loose your job.

A recovery is when Obama looses his job."

We must be sure that Obama is only a one term President. His actions and his response to our concerns should be top priority. As we all know, we are not on his agenda when it comes to organizing our Nation even if he does have organizing experience.

He's like a kid in a candy store when it comes to our money. He is unable to budget our Nations monetary issues. It would help if he quit using our money like it was his own personal bank account. He just throws money around like there is no end to it. How much more of our money will it take for Obama to have paid back everyone from his campaign promises? It's not easy to think that our tax dollars were and are being spent for Obama's election.

What about the lawmakers travel budget money? They are allotted $250.00 a day when traveling out of the Country. The real kicker here is, they don't have to show any receipts for anything nor is there any kind of record for money spent. So if they don't spend all of the daily allowance they can pocket the money or buy something unrelated to their travel expense. This is unbelievable. They should have to account for every dime spent and any left over should be returned back. This is quite the scam. Who needs that kind of money per day? It sure leaves a bad taste in my mouth to know that our tax payer money is also funding these added extras.

Have you noticed how our lawmakers are starting to get caught in their lies? Pelosi stated she was not aware of water boarding. Low and Behold, she was aware of this procedure. She had to of felt like a jerk getting caught in that lie.

What about lawmaker Mr. Wrangler, he has enjoyed a Caribbean trip and many other goodies that they are not suppose to accept. And gee, he didn't know where it came from. If some one sent you on a free trip, wouldn't you want to know who the kind soul was that paid for it? How does Mr. Wrangler get away with out claiming rental money income and back taxes? We could not get away with such a thing. We would be charged interest, fined and maybe go to jail. But I forgot, it's okay to be crooked and cheat when you are representative of our Nation. It's not hard to understand why he has taken time off. He just wanted to get out of the lime light, so no more attention would be drawn toward him, you know out of sight, out of mind.

Due to a microphone being left on at the Blair House in the garden room, our Vice President Joe Bieden stated "that it was easy being Vice President because he didn't have to do anything" and agreed that it was like being a grandparent and not the parent. Well, who the hell does he think he is? We expect a little more out of our V.P. than that. If his job is so easy and such little of work to be done, than Obama should delegate more work his way. Anyone in that kind of position should have many responsibilities and be busy as hell. But we heard it from the horse's mouth. He is useless in office and should not be there.

Another bothersome tid bit of information is that there are about ten Communists working within our Congress. Why are we allowing this to happen? Obama is allowing these positions to be filled by Communist and we are supposed to live with this arrangement. Where is our security at when it comes to interviewing these people? Or, perhaps they aren't even checked out. They just fill positions with Communist, Fascists, Radicals and who ever else they feel like sleeping with. Our Country is going to hell in a hand basket and Obama is leading the way.

Do you realize that Congress has not taken a cut in pay for 77 years? Don't you agree that it is about time they do take a cut in pay to help out with the economic crisis that we are in? A Congress woman from Arizona came up with a good idea. If all of Congress took a 5% pay cut, it would save about 46 million dollars. Wow that would help. As a matter of fact let's make Congress take that pay cut and divide it amongst the Americans to pay off some of their debt. You know redistribute the wealth....After all she is taking a 5% cut herself and deserves a pat on the back, so all you Arizonians should be proud of your Congress woman.

Obama continues to make poor decisions while he is in office. Can you imagine that the man he put in charge to create jobs is the same man that does not believe in Free Market? Now how the hell is a man that doesn't believe in free market going to help out our economy if he doesn't believe in it? It doesn't take a rocket scientist to figure that one out either.

Then there is Andy Stern who was ahead of S.E.I.U. Obama is consulting with him on the job problem in America. Please tell us this is not true. Obama is going to take advice from a man who has lost the pension funds within his organization. The Unions and Obama have been sleeping together since his campaign. Now Obama owes him so many favors for all the money they invested in him. If you're really wondering why Obama owes our Unions, it's because they gave him 100 million dollars for his campaign.

The worst part about this is that we Americans are going to suffer during this payback time. Of course this will be done on a favoritism agenda. What ever the Unions want they will get because Obama owes them. So with knowing all this, would you agree that Andy Stern is the last person Obama should be consulting with? For some reason these two want to change the World. They probably hope to Unionize the entire World. If or when this happens, our jobs will really suck. The unions will want more dues and expect us to be at their mercy. We must recognize this as a possibility and reframe from being taken in by their tactics. Unions only protect the bad workers and the good workers don't need them. We all should consider abolishing the Unions forever.

Isn't it amazing how we all pay our Social Security taxes, and yet the government has spent our money. Our pension funds have been gambled away. That is why it is so important for our monies to be put in special accounts that the government can not touch.

We do not need them playing retirement roulette with our money. As we get older our retirement is very important to us. After all, we are too old to continue working. We all pay into our Social Security just so we have that back up when we get too old to work. And now the government wants to basically say I'm sorry but we blew your money so "oh well." Just what in hell, are we suppose to do? It really does tend to give us an attitude toward the government when they steal from us.

Obama and his sidekicks have come up with a new phrase called Social Justice. But to explain it in a nut shell is easy. It is forcibly redistributing the wealth. The key word there is forcibly. Do we want to be forced to do something we don't want to do?

If Congress thinks we don't like the wording of something, as usual they will just change it, hoping to confuse us. We can not and will not accept Social Justice into our lives. This might be okay for the Communists and Socialists that are in office now, but it is not going to be our new way of life. That is not living. That is being told what to do, when they say so.

With the government running HUD, they have spent 65 billion dollars on public housing rental subsides. We need to consider getting a financial advisor for our Whitehouse and Congress. Not one, which they choose, but one that America votes on. Someone who will say no to all spending not related to the functions of the Whitehouse and Congress.

The Senate wants to raise the gasoline tax again, something to do with the unveiling of their new Climate Bill. If we drilled for our own damn oil we would not have to count on the foreign Countries and our gas prices would be a whole lot less. This is the most important issue that Congress will ever have and they can not come through for us. This does not and will never make any sense.

The government is going to put a stronger hold on us yet, because the FCC is going to make the Internet a public utility. That means the government will regulate it, as it is trying to regulate and rule every thing in our life. It is happening slowly but quickly if you know what I mean. We are all going to feel the pain when they get their claws wrapped around us. I don't think any of us really know what is happening to our world. But I do know that we will not favor the outcome.

It looks like someone in our government is trying very hard to collapse the economy of the world. If that happens and we all find ourselves going hungry due to no money for food, it will be the perfect chance for our government to step in and act like our savior. When all along this is what they have been trying to do. We can not allow ourselves to rely on the government for help and support. This is what they want and are striving for.

We must remain strong and self sufficient in order to control our future happiness and freedom.

You can almost see it happening now. They are trying to take away our Miranda rights, giving them more control yet. They want to be able to see what you have in your private bank account, which is no business of theirs. It's like the consumer shake down. They are gaining more control over our personal life and accounts. Now they want to look into your charge cards and see what you have been charging on your accounts. Who the hell are they to dig into our personal life? How do you feel about them knowing what you're doing and how you're doing it? It's our business if we charge a pair of socks and a battery for our car. This just isn't right. Our freedom is no longer ours. We can not continue to call it freedom. It's basically existence by government approval. Wake Up every body what's yours will not be yours much longer, that extra TV you have in your bedroom will soon be taken from you and sent to another Country and given to someone else who doesn't have one. You know, share the wealth, after you busted your ass to make enough money to have that extra TV, now Obama wants you to share it, no second thought he wants you to give it up for some asshole who sits around and does nothing and cries that he goes with out. Not much good can be said about a man that would ask you to give up what you worked hard to get.

Obama does not like it if you make too much money. He has said many times that an individual doesn't need to make so much money. But yet he is involved in many money making schemes and still making millions of dollars, and we should wonder just how he gets away with all this. It is legal in his eyes, but with him being a lawyer and all, he knows the way to back door these schemes and makes it look legit. Don't we wish we could do that? When you really think about it he is a very scary man, because he can't be trusted, he will not listen to we the people, he is linked to many outside groups that money goes right from our hand into his, and he is out to destroy our economy and our freedom. Just think, many of you voted him in to do this to us. That phrase: "How do you Like That Hopey Changey Thing?" Is quite the question, a little sarcastic but truly stated.

We should have many concerns about our land here in the United States. Right now the government owns at least 33% of the land in the U.S. which is way too much. Our government is abusing the Eminent Domain law and doing a huge land grab from many land owners right in front of our faces. There is not a damn thing we can do about it either. Now what kind of government did we elect, that would treat us like this?

Here is a good laugh for Americans; Congress decides to hold a meeting to curve some of the wasteful spending, which of course is well needed. But instead of holding the meeting at the Whitehouse, they rent the Ritz Carlton in Arizona for their meeting. Someone please tell me what ignorant soul chose the most expensive hotel there is, to hold their meeting at. How stupid are they? This is ridiculous and not acceptable. This has to be a joke. We are trusting in these people to get our Country back on track and they do this. WOW, you do the math.

My second favorite is Pelosi's accomplishment party. Even though 70% of Americans have been against all their decision making with the Health Care Bill and other bills, she decides to celebrate all that they have accomplished with a big bash. Gee, ever wonder who paid for this party? What a great way to cut wasteful spending.

Are you aware that a Supreme Court Judge has a life time position? This is crazy. Why would any position in our government have a ruling that once elected as a Supreme Court Judge you would hold that job until you quit or die? This really needs to be looked into. No position held in our government should be forever. It's bad enough we can't trust them, so it's important that a Judge does not stay in a position long enough to turn crooked, which obviously doesn't take long to happen.

It's amazing how Obama says he does not like theatrical politics, but he uses them more than any President has. Remember the Health Care Bill that he has pushed down our throats? Well he had people wearing Doctor's smocks during the discussions as the media took pictures. Then when Obama was signing the bill he had a child there, so we could see just how much this bill would help the children. As you can see, he did use theatrical in his political issues, not counting many others that Americans just don't notice? Why does Obama say one thing and do the other? I can't describe how frustrating his lies have become to us.

The cabinet members in Congress consist of Democrats and Republicans of course, and Obama deals with these members all the time. The strange thing about it is that there are about six cabinet members that he hasn't even spoke to in two years. Talk about lack of communication. Why is it that these members have not talked to our President? We must be concerned with Obama's strange behavior within the political world. It seems he only associates with individuals who he will benefit from. Too bad Obama supports the Unions so strongly; it causes others in our government to be less effective.

In 2009 Obama received billions of dollars from Egypt for the sale of weapons. Why would we sell weapons to another Country? This does not make any sense. Doesn't that weaken our military and strengthen the foreign side of the World? We must object to the sale of any of our military weapons, equipment and supplies or vehicles including planes, if these are of no use to us then they should be destroyed, not sold to other Countries to further their power of destruction. Some way some how these items will be used against us. You can bet on that.

It's amazing how our politicians think. One of them said in the middle of a disaster, "Never let a good crisis go by". That is terrible to think that our government would take advantage of someone or something in the middle of a crisis. As each day goes by it is getting easier to see why our Nation is being turned upside down.

A word of advice to Congress would be, nothing ever gets done without a deadline. But I am sure they won't abide by that saying. That's a little to ethical for them.

Chapter 13............Politically Incorrect

It sounds like the saying Politically Incorrect is something about politics that you perhaps didn't understand or you spoke about it in the wrong context. But it does not mean that at all. It is really about defining someone, such as, calling an African American a black person. How does a person really know what to call people? Are they black, African American, or Negro? What does this race like being called? What is Politically Correct?

Many people get into trouble when speaking because of the uncertainty of what to call people. We know that a slang term for an African American is Nigger, which of course is improper, morally and politically incorrect. It should not be so hard to figure out what to call people with out worrying about offending them. The same holds true for Mexicans. Do you say Hispanics, brown people,

Mexicans or what? We all seem to know the slang or improper name to call different races but we really don't know what they desire or want. This could go on and on with many of the different races.

Now days, people are too sensitive to their race. What ever happened to telling jokes?

There were blonde jokes, black jokes, Mexican, Polish, and so on. But the humor seemed to disappear as the sensitivity got higher with these racial jokes. The fact that these racial jokes tend to offend people tells us that maybe they are ashamed of their race. Where did our humor go? Why is it that we can't be content enough to speak as we wish?

Laughter has become a thing of the past. We don't take time to smell the flowers anymore. Everything is made a big deal out of. I don't care what color your skin is, there is bad and good in every race. Some races have reputations that aren't as good as others. Perhaps that's because the minority has ruined it for those who are decent.

It has always been hard to live up to other peoples expectations. But on the other hand just why in hell do we have to? Freedom of speech should dominate and therefore make it okay to say what we feel even if it is politically incorrect.

Who determines if something is politically incorrect? Is it our government? I don't think so, or rather we should hope not. What is strange is that people of different races always use their race against us. All we have to do is say something they don't like and we become Racists. How fair is that? Well just because you say something about someone does not make you a Racist. Perhaps the different races in this world should grow up and leave things alone and quit blaming others for all their failures and insecurities.

This is America; we don't owe any body any apologies for being an American. We are proud of our Country and are willing to accept anyone who is interested in becoming an American as long as they play by our rules and not theirs. We are the freest Nation in the World. At least up to this point.

It tends to bother me that people come to America and want to change our rules and try to manipulate our beliefs. If you aren't happy here then by all means, leave. We do not need citizens in our Country that are ashamed of America or feel they have to protest our laws. What you see, is what you get.

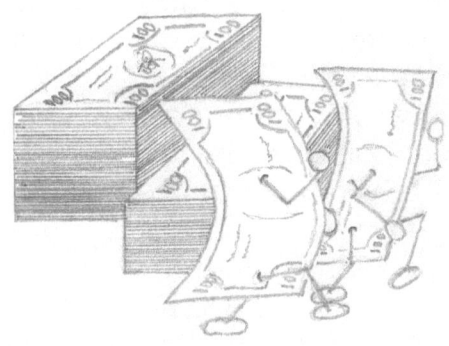

Chapter 14 .... Our Money

We should touch base with where billions of our dollars are going. Do you know? Are you paying attention to what all this borrowed money is being spent on? Do you care? Because you better wake up and check out just what our government is blowing our money on.

For starters, do you realize that they spent 4.4 million dollars for the teachers in the public schools in North Carolina to learn how to teach school? What.......?

Isn't that why they hired them because they are teachers and they have a degree in teaching? This is absolutely unacceptable. This is an outrage. Those 4.4 million dollars would have prolonged our Social Security problems and helped out thousands of citizens. How stupid does this make Congress look?

Another study for plant fossils has received 1.5 million dollars in Argentina. But it did create three American jobs. Ooh... When is 1.5 million dollars okay to spend just to create three jobs? We should fire everyone who signed this bill into effect including every body that okayed all these millions of dollars to be spent.

California received $383,000.00 to send their teachers and administrators to a Hollywood spa, and felt it was more important then spending the money for school supplies. Now we know why California is broke and doing very badly. Can you imagine this wasteful spending? It makes you laugh with how incredible this outrage is. They also received another $233,000.00 to the University of California to study why Africans vote. Get Real Congress. You are really starting to make us angry.

Arizona received 1 million for the study of ants. What are we thinking? Although, I did mention this in another chapter, the million spent for this is crazy.

Then there is Nevada who built fire stations for 2 million dollars and then due to budget cuts they can't afford to pay wages for firemen to use them. They sure did some prior proper planning for this program Huh? Are you aware that our government officials are on the internet surfing porno sites while they are at work and we pay them to do so? These officials that are involved in these kinds of work habits need to be put on suspension and watched a little closer. If they spent more time reading our bills and less time playing on the internet, perhaps we would not be in the shape were in. This obviously isn't classified information if our cabinet members are looking at skin flicks. Someone better do something about this bad habit by our government officials. Where in hell do you get off doing this, anyone else would be fired?

Can you believe the government spent 4 million dollars on weatherizing only 47 homes? You could build 200 homes with that kind of money. Who did the work? Who ever is responsible for these jobs better be real glad the government chose them as opposed to someone else. I bet who ever did it was in coo hoots with some government official. This is just ridiculous, it makes me so angry to see our money just go to waste like that. If we don't stop this outrageous spending we will be in big trouble. What the hell is wrong with Obama? He is aware of all this and just continues to put us deeper in debt. Obama needs to be released from office and the sooner the better. We will be much better off when his term is up.

Obama stated that he was going to put a spending freeze on the Whitehouse, but that won't be until another year. In the meantime, we will be so broke there won't be any money to spend so therefore, no money will be spent. He is only saying that he won't spend anymore money than he already has. Well if we're about 4 trillion dollars in debt he is right, he won't be able to spend more than he has in his first year as President. No President in history has ever spent this much money or put us in such a critical situation. He is putting us in danger of loosing our Country while he destroys our Nation. Obama is an individual that appears to be ignorant of our situation or perhaps chooses to ignore it, because that is his mission to seek out and destroy America by what ever means it takes. Any President that doesn't know how many states are in the United States should not be the Commander in Chief. A President should know how many states we have within our Nation.

His idea of closing Guantanamo Bay is just more wasteful spending. It is shocking to hear that he has changed his mind and will not close Guantanamo at this time. We have spent millions of dollars to set the place up for terrorist trials. It's good to hear that he doesn't want to move the prisoners to another area in the states. It really wasn't necessary. We have spent enough money on these Terrorists. Bringing them to New York for trial would of cost us more money and would be a big inconvenience for New York. No body wants these Terrorists in their state. By them moving them to the states also gives them more rights and believe me,

Terrorists do not need any rights from our Country. Many have died and suffered because of them and because of Obama, they still continue to haunt us. Some thing is not right about this situation. Someone is paying off someone to accommodate these prisoners. We will probably never find out. But be assured, something is not right.

As we all know the war in Iraq has cost us a fortune. But leaving equipment there is not wise. Why are we leaving Hummers and miscellaneous equipment there for the Iraq's to use or study them to come back and harm us in the future? This makes no sense. This equipment is too expensive to just leave there. This is just another waste of our hard earned money. We took them to Iraq, and we must bring them all back. With the economy being so bad, this is not the time to be wasteful. They say it is cheaper to leave the equipment there than to bring it back. I just can't imagine that.

Look at the floods along the E. Coast, such as Connecticut, Rhode Island and Massachusetts. It's in question whether we should help pay for them to rebuild. It's great to help out other states, but damn it, don't build a home in the middle of a flood area. Why should we give them our hard earned tax dollars just so they can rebuild and then have it happen again when the next flood comes? It doesn't take a rocket scientist to figure that one out.

They want to spend over 40 billion dollars to depopulate the Mississippi Coast and part of Louisiana, if they would just leave things alone, people could not afford to rebuild and they would eventually move else where. So why is it that they feel the need to waste all this money?

Do you remember how our money went for those Mortgage bailouts? Well majority of the people that were bailed out are still in default even after their mortgage was paid up. So we might as well have taken all those billions of dollars and burned it up.

The way our government handles our money is like a ponzi scheme. They continue to keep spending but do not have the funds to do so. They just add zero's here and there and change the amounts and then use it somewhere else like the money is there and it is NOT!

Do you realize how much of our money is wasted on unused flight tickets? Yes, there is almost 100 million dollars in tickets that someone in Congress failed to cancel their said trips and neglected to get the flight ticket refunded to them. The money didn't come out of their pockets so they aren't worried about a refund of any money. This is terrible to see how they waste more of our money. Words can't even express it at this point.

Why does the government pay farmers not to grow things? What reasoning is there behind this? We should not be paid not to grow things. We should be encouraged to grow as much as possible to strengthen our food source Nation wide. It's just another chunk out of our paycheck. Perhaps many of us could tolerate some of this spending if there was just a legitimate reason to be doing so.

The errors that the government makes is totaling an all time high. Because they send out many kinds of different checks, they have wasted 72 billion dollars on improper payments. Gee, I wonder how many animals have gotten a check. Perhaps, grandma or grandpa died and they did not report it to the government, so one of the relatives just keeps signing the checks and spending the money.

It seriously is one thing to get a little extravagant when spending money, however Obama's three day trip to London is ridiculous. He took 500 people on his trip. Approximately 200 secret service agents, who in hell needs that many people to watch their back, unless you have something to worry about, second thought, after seeing how he is destroying America, maybe he does need that many. Then he took the Whitehouse chef and all kitchen staff including his own food and water. Who in their right mind would take that many people for a 3 day trip? Wouldn't it have been cheaper to eat out for those 3 days? He also took six Doctors. Why would you need that many Doctor's? Sounds like he doesn't trust his own staff of Doctor's, he just wants to take oodles and oodles of Doctor's in case he gets a Boo Boo. The ridiculous part of all this is, he brought 35 vehicles for a three day venture which included a helicopter and the Presidential limo. Why? Someone please tell us Americans a really good reason to justify this. The money it took to fund this three day trip is outrageous. Words can not describe the idiotic decisions for this trip. No body in this whole World should be able to do this. This is not acceptable to us Americans. Mr. Obama shame on you, who the hell do you think you are? You're just wasting our hard earned money.

Oh then, there was 12 teleprompters and 4 speech writers. It's hard to believe that Obama went to college and he needs all this. This disgusts me to no end. It is hard to stop thinking about the money this President just blows that comes out of our pockets.

We must put a stop to his evil spending. This is our money not his. There has never been a President that has spent this kind of money and yet he can still sleep at night and wake up the next day and tell us another lie or two. This is not right or fair for our own President to be so wasteful. It seems I mentioned wasteful so many times, but we need to drill this in to our heads so that we understand exactly what is happening.

It seems Michelle Obama is following in his footsteps; she has now hired her own personal shopper. Come on, really, doesn't she have time to do her own damn shopping? After all she does not work. The most puzzling thing about this is who's paying for this? Do you suppose it is out of her allowance? Of course not, we the taxpayer's are footing the bill. Doesn't this just make you jump for joy?

It is really hard to swallow, when you see the government abusing every dime that they take out of our paycheck. If you still had that 25% of your check, you might have been able to buy some extra groceries or put gas in the car so you didn't have to worry about having enough gas to get to work on. You can best believe Michelle is not worried where her next dime is coming from.

When it comes to Foreign Aid, John Kerry wants to send more of our money to the Arab World. We spend billions of dollars a year sending other Countries money and now he wants to increase it. Well Bull____. I refuse to hear this. It has to be a mistake. Just think he was running for President once upon a time. All of our money would be going to other Countries and we would be cutting back in our Country to fund theirs. It is Our Money and I will repeat, Our Money that these jerks are playing games with.

After 96 members of the cabinet were voted out and departing the house, that also put each member's staff out of a job. Each one of these members is given 2 million dollars a year to help them and their staff to operate. I must say 192 million dollars is a big junk of cash out of the budget and our money. If any of the 2 million dollars is left then it is supposed to be given back. Guess what? These members decided to give their staff a bonus since they were loosing their jobs, so with the 6.7 million dollars that was left they split it between all the staff members. This really grinds my ass. This money is ours and we did not okay anyone to receive such a bonus. We need this 6.7 million and I can not understand why Obama would let these people get away with this. Obama seems to think our money is his to just squander away and doesn't care if an extra little tid bit like 6 million is gone. It's no wonder our Nation is broke. There is no fiscal control in Congress.

When speaking of being out of control, our Federal Reserve System has abused their power long enough. It is time to have them audited. It is a crime the way they manipulate our money. It's really hard to believe that these people get away with doing whatever floats their boat. The Federal Reserve was created by an act of Congress and can be abolished by an act of Congress. Our very own President doesn't even have any say so when it comes to the Federal Reserve, which is not a good policy.

Chapter 15........................ Stimulus Bill

How about the new wording on this bill? It makes Congress feel better to call a Stimulus bill a Jobs bill. Obama is hoping that we don't put the two together. Let's face it, a Jobs bill or a Stimulus bill is still the same, just another version of spending more of our money. We have a problem though; this trillion dollar Stimulus has an interest rate of a 100 million a day. Yes you read that right. Just how are we to ever pay this back? Just hearing this should make us sick to our stomachs. We basically are screwed; we will never see daylight again, thanks to our sneaky, lying, deceiving, arrogant, and wasteful spending President.

We have 11 million people out of work and it's costing the government about 1.5 million for every 3 jobs they create. At this rate it will take a life time to put half of the people back to work. It's just not going to happen. It's just another excuse to blow our money. Jobs can be created and workers can find different sources of employment, but not by Obama's way.

It's hard to believe that he talks of saving a job. If a job is there and being filled by a worker, then how in hell is he saving this job? How stupid do they think we are? Saving a job does not count for anything. The amount of jobs that Obama has created is ridiculously low. Where does he get off trying to convince us, of his greatness? The Tea Party has probably created more jobs in six months than Obama has in over a year.

One tax that is a conversation piece is a tax credit. They make it sound like they just put thousands of dollars in your pocket. These tax credits are only handy for a few people and are no use to the majority of the population. Yes, they want to give tax credits for first time home buyers. That is a very small percentage of the population. Most people have bought several homes and many can't afford to.

But you never see any tax credits for the majority of people. You either have to be a student, have 10 kids, or buy a home. Why can't they ever offer more people a variety of tax credits so that we may all get a break? But no, because the government wants to make themselves look good, and yet still not give us any breaks that will help.

Soon they will be taking fees out of our checks instead of taxes. Does it really matter what they call the deductions? They still come out of our check. Do they really think we will feel better being charged fees instead of taxes?

What will people do without jobs? There would be more jobs if the government quit taxing a business so much money. After paying these taxes there is no extra money for wages. We must give the business owners more tax breaks which will create more jobs. After all, when is the last time a poor person offered you a job? It's just not going to happen. Therefore we must help business owners out in order for the economy to pick up. Taxes are important, but they don't have to devour our paycheck.

The government spending is so out of control that there is no light at the end of the tunnel. Perhaps we would see a shadow of some light if those boys on Capital Hill would start taking concessions and curve their spending habits.

It's time to start cutting back on government employees. We can start by getting rid of all of Obama's Czars. They are an added expense in payroll and are not needed. We have never had to use Czars before and they need to be dismissed. Next we need to look at the unnecessary spending done within the Whitehouse and Capital Hill. Their cafeteria or dinner area should be looked into. There should be simple meals on the menu and not extravagant dishes like there is now. The Speaker of the House gets to decide what goes on the menu. So the blame can start there. Pelosi had way to many expensive food choices on the menu. Perhaps John Boehner can do a better job. They don't need to eat like that at work. Do we? No.

Our Congress members are treated like kings and this must stop. No more bonus's for government officials. When it comes time for their vacation, they are not to use the tax payer's money for jet fuel to travel back and forth. Pelosi is one to abuse the usage of our jets. This has to stop. She and all others can pay for their own transportation. We also foot many bills for the relatives of our government officials. This is not fair to us taxpayers.

The expenses' that the President and his family incur are another burden to our debt. No more lavish spending. Every dime that goes out of that Whitehouse is coming out of our pocket and not the President's. He receives a pay check just like everyone else; therefore he can afford to pay many expenses that he and his family create that we don't like paying for.

It's bad enough that they want to bail out every Tom, Dick and Harry that their in bed with, but this also must stop. Let these companies fail. That is what life's all about. We don't need Fanny Mae and Freddy Mac and who ever, maybe Froggy Woggy, who knows. We just need to stop giving them money, only to fail again down the road.

There are other Financial Institutes that will step up to the plate and take off where Fanny Mae failed.

It seems like when the government needs something done they don't get estimates or shop around for a better cheaper deal. Why is this? We all do. Why do they have to hire the most expensive company out there? I know for a fact, that all that they have done from gardeners to auto mechanics that I could hire someone to do the job for half the price they pay. You see, they just don't give a damn about saving any money to help out our economy. Their selfish and extremist's and think that because there is billions of dollars coming from us that they can squander it away. It is time to vote them out and bring in the new.

They are setting aside 75 million dollars out of the Jobs Bill to help bail out chicken farmers. Do you realize for only a few million you can buy all sorts of chicken farms and start over again? I'm sure that these farmers need help, but let's be real, enough of these million dollar bailouts.

Let's not forget about the other 21 million dollars being set aside, from this same Job's Bill for the sugar cane crops in Hawaii. Wow, where do we get this kind of money from? Why are we, as Americans struggling every day of our lives and some are looking for jobs and yet they blow our tax payer money on this kind of garbage? I suppose we could look at it like the government would be saving jobs. But it would almost be cheaper to create new jobs than to spend that kind of money.

There have been as many as 469,000 new claims for unemployment and it changes daily. What can we do to better our situation? It is plain to see that Congress is not going to help the job market. We must do it ourselves. It is so important to take the stress off of the companies and business's in order for them to put people back to work. How can Congress demand such harsh rules for these companies without expecting some kind of reaction to the economy? By extending everyone's unemployment compensation, it is helpful but with such long extensions it tends to make people live off that instead of looking for a job. The funds will run out and the problem will still be there.

With over 15 million people out of work and over 11 million are on some kind of jobless benefit, the economy will go into a recession that could lead to a depression. When we have reliable people in the Whitehouse and Congress, times seem to pick up and get better. So this is our cue, the people that we have voted in have to go. They are not good for the future of our economy. Too many people are out of work. It really stems back to how the business owners are getting gouged by the government with taxes and more taxes. We need to give more breaks to the businesses in order to stimulate our economy. They truly are the backbone to our Nation.

In order for economic growth, the Stimulus should have been handled differently and distributed in a better way. It was a waste of money and used improperly. Stimulus for government workers is not a good foundation for our future. This Stimulus bill was basically created to take money from the rich and give to the poor. They put 900 billion dollars in to that bill. That is so much money for such little results. Soon the wealthier will be carrying the load. That is not going to go over very well with the rich.

By extending Unemployment Benefits to 99 weeks, it has made for endless hand outs. This creates dependency by counting on these checks and does not help job productivity. We must quit relying on the government for help. They want us in a weakened, state, so please find a job and go to work. The more helpless we are, the more the government will have over you. Any help needed should be with state and local agencies, we must keep the federal away from us. When you're at their mercy is when times will get harder and it will make it easier for them to control us.

We need to avoid government hand outs. We do not want to become a nanny state, where the government takes care of us. That just gives them more control and power over us. It looks like that's what the government wants and that's why they really aren't doing anything about our job situation. Many Hi Tech jobs are leaving our Country because there is no incentive for these businesses's to stay here. Obama seems to think that most businesses are corrupt. That's a joke coming from Mr. Corrupt 101. You can not raise the businesses taxes so high that they leave our Country. But maybe that's what Obama wants; they want us jobless and in need of government help.

We now have another Stimulus called American Jobs and closing Tax loopholes act of 2010. Obama knew we would not go for another Jobs Bill so he come up with this one, thinking we were dumb enough not to figure out that it's just more money for the same damn thing. His idea of a job is also a joke. He thinks it takes 10 million dollars to create 5 jobs. How sick is this? Who is the dumb one? That's about as stupid as them funding a research program on why monkey's like Doritos's when their high on cocaine. This makes about as much sense as the Job/ Stimulus programs.

The big company's out there are hoarding their money instead of hiring people. They are scared of what could happen next. After all they didn't get to be a big boy by making bad choices. The job market is getting worse because companies are running scared. Fear holds people back. No one can feel comfortable with an unstable government that spends more than they have.

The other day I received a letter in the mail, after opening it I could not believe my eyes. It was in regards to a two million dollar private hearing Stimulus announced for Michigan. It stated that over a million people have hearing loss that affects their quality of life. Included was a voucher for $1000.00 to be used for hearing aids. At first I didn't think much about it because I have good hearing, however, after some deep thought I realized that this was more of our tax payer dollars being distributed out in voucher form. As I read further on it stated that this was not part of a government sponsored benefit or bailout and does not have to be repaid. My thoughts ended in well who the hell is paying for this then? I really think it was some company who was trying to take advantage of the word Stimulus and use it as an advertising ploy. I thought it stunk and was uncalled for.

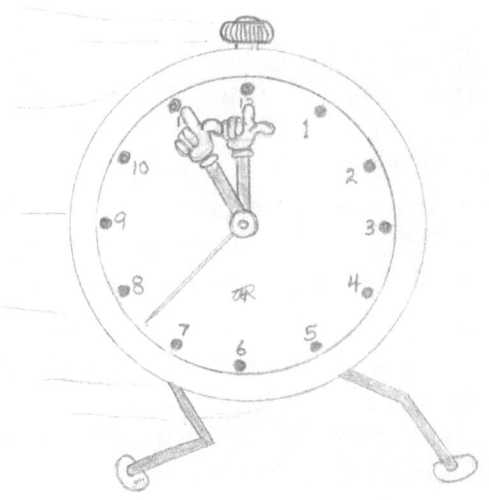

Chapter 16 ....It's Time

The United States of America has always been a free and proud Country. We have always held our heads up high and aimed for the sky. We take pride in our Country and offer many lands aide and understanding. When ever another Country needed help we were always there with help and money. We have rebuilt many Nations and stood by their side. We have donated our time, our efforts and our tax payer dollars to do well unto others.

But now it's time. It's time for us to understand that our Nation has become weaker, more vulnerable and insecure. We can no longer be the big shoulder that everyone tends to rely on. We no longer have the funds to be a nice guy anymore. Not if we want to maintain our reputation, our freedom and our dignity. It's time to tighten up our shoe strings to become the strong Nation we once were.

It's not a matter of change, but a matter of resorting back to our proud Nation once again. To do this we must admit to ourselves that we are in trouble. Look around at what is happening. Do things still seem to be the same? Why are there groups like Tea Parties getting together? This tells us that it's time to clean up our act. The government is choosing to ignore the desperation that we are in. Why are they doing this? They are suppose to be our leaders, look out for our best interest, promote our well being and protect us all. None of this is remotely close to what we are receiving from our government. With that in mind we must resort to looking out for ourselves.

Should we be preparing for rough times? What kind of rough times? Is the government becoming our enemy? Gee let's hope not. Should we be stock piling food? Who can afford to do that? We barely can make ends meet now let alone spending extra money on stock piling food or whatever. This sucks. What is a person suppose to do? We could all wait for the disaster to hit and worry about it then. But that's a little scary, wouldn't you say? How does a person store fuel, food and money? It's almost impossible unless you're very wealthy. We must find a way to save ourselves from the mistakes that our government is making with our tax dollars. Our decision in the next couple of years is what's going to save our ass. We must study our politicians that are running for office. We must interrogate them to the utmost. They must be the right person to replace the monsters we have in there now. That is our only survival, our only hope and the only way that we can save ourselves from this government's behavior.

We are the decision makers in our Country; we are the strong ones and the leaders of our own civilization. It's up to us to follow the path with the least destruction lead by individuals that are strong, honest, and reliable and the stamina to make the right decisions for all of us. Obviously no one fits that description on Capital Hill right now.

We must stop sending money to these other Countries for them to rebuild their Nation. No more grants and special funds for nonsense things. Put a stop to educational grants until we become strong again. They are important but we have to cut costs and the time is now. Foolish grants such as the study of different animals, fossils and etc. need to be discontinued. As we grow strong again we can then consider these trivial pursuits.

The only fund at this time that is probably a very important one would be a Natural Disaster Fund. We never know what Mother Nature wants to bring our way. Many people are devastated by hurricanes, earthquakes and tornados. Some towns are completely torn apart at no fault of their own. They do need help until they can get back on their feet. But this help would be for our Country only, no one else. We can not be kind to others any longer. Our Nation is suffering now so we must take care of our own.

The millions of dollars that our government has just blown are so upsetting that words can no longer describe our feelings toward this. The war is also costing us too much money so it's time to get it over with. If we don't protect our wealth and our people as soon as possible, then the terrorists will have an upper hand.

There was a time in my life where I could have cared less about the politicians or Congress or the President. But as we age, our lifestyle changes, and there are more concerns about many things that didn't mean a hill of beans. My only hope for the many of Americans out there now is that they pay more attention to what's going on because it is so important to our life and more so for our children who will have to struggle because of our neglect with politics.

Our children and our grand children will live a very poor life if we don't stop all the spending, the bribes and the lies in Congress right now. We must stand up for our beliefs and demand satisfaction for a better America, a safer Country and respect from our leaders in hopes they will listen to us and see that we are not happy with them.

We all have our own religious beliefs, regardless of what kind of religion it may be. But I truly think that the only thing that will save our Country is the belief in God, it will be a strength that will conquer all. Many people believe in God and that belief tends to bring out the good in people. It is hard to understand why the government wants to deprive us of our beliefs. There are some who do not believe in God. But they still believe in themselves and therefore they too, also have a belief. So, having beliefs and trust in something or someone will be a stronger weapon than anyone can imagine. Having faith in what a person believes in will be the savior of our Country. You don't necessarily need to believe in God, but just believing in ones self will be our government's enemy.

It's time for us to be strong in our thinking, strong with our decisions and strong willed enough to tolerate our government's poor judgment and preposterous spending. We can and we will do this. We are stronger than any government could possibly be. We all want and need rules and guidance, but it would be nice if our concerns were addressed and not dismissed.

We must not put ourselves in the position where the government is taking care of us. If this happens more rules will come our way. Food will be scarce and housing will be for the rich only. We need leaders, not dictators. We need men with backbones, not rubber lips. We need new ideas followed by encouragement, not new laws followed by fines and beatings. We need a political system that has strength to freeze spending and knows right from wrong and not someone who is out for themselves and to hell with what happens to all of us Americans. Why is it so hard to find this? What do we have to do to find leaders that are willing to listen to us as people instead of trying to change our World?

Our Country is losing more and more business's each year. We must put an end to this loss. Without business's small or large, the world will eat it's self up. The only thing that keeps prices at an even keel is the competition of each business. Competition is the best regulator. It keeps our costs in check. With so many of them going out of business, it creates a monopoly and causes prices to soar out of hand. It's the little guy that keeps the ball rolling and it's them that we need to give some tax breaks to. We do not want to put the small businesses on the endangered species list. We must not turn our backs on free trade.

It's truly time to do away with many of our problems. Our biggest problem that seems to always slap us in the face is the Unions. Do you realize how much power these people have over us? We need to demolish all Unions. There was a time when they were needed for employee's rights, however that time is over. I am sure you are aware that the man behind all of the Unions is George Soros. He is not a kind old man. He is evil and backs many committee's, companies and agencies with all his billions of dollars. He is the one man that wants a global government and is working very hard to destroy our Nation.

Beware of his dealings, for he is the root of all evil. Money always seems to talk and this man has enough of that to keep up a conversation for a life time. As Glen Beck would say "The Spooky Dude". Yes he is. The scary thing about him is all his money and power. Not too many people can touch this man. Don't you just hate someone with that kind of power? He must be stopped from trying to make us a Global government. We do not want any part of a Global anything. We do not want to loose our Nation. We are the United States of America and no one or other Country shall take us over or tell us what to do. We must stand our ground. We must not let money and power destroy our Nation.

We must be prepared for many changes and some of them we are not going to be happy with. What should bother us deeply is why would Obama be speaking with this man? What could they possibly have to talk about or have in common? Perhaps Obama has the same agenda as Mr. Soros. If this so be the case, we better make sure Obama never serves another term in office. We do not need a man with Global Government on his mind or in his future plans. It is bad enough that Obama speaks of Global this, and Global that. We are the ones that better get our minds together and read between the lines and hear what our government is really saying. They have a way of wording things that tend to float right over our head. But if you stopped and deciphered each paragraph that they state, we would be surprised with what they really mean and what their intentions really are.

It's time to do something about this problem with top secret documents being taken off the web site Wikki leaks. Yes someone is stealing top notch goodies from our government and nothing is being done to prevent it. Why is our secret data from the Whitehouse's computers so easy to access that someone can go in to it and find out things that could hurt our Country? Don't we hire top notch people to make sure that this info is not leaked out to just anyone? This should bother us very deeply. The fact that someone is possibly selling our Country's secrets such as military maneuvers or weapons or anything that we do not want another Country to get their hands on is more than just scary, it's horrendous.

As stated many times, we must stop all Foreign Aid, because other Countries are using and abusing our generosity. Take Egypt for example, we have been giving them billions of dollars and now we find out that the Dictator of Egypt may be pocketing all that money for his own personal use. This money was supposed to be for the Country and their people, not just one man to hoard it all.

Just recently I heard that the only reason we give aid to these Foreign Countries is basically a pay off to them for our safety from them. What? Do you mean to tell me, that all these billions of dollars of our money are going for mainly bribes and protection? This is America, why do we fear other Countries? Why does our Nation's safety depend on us paying them to leave us alone? This is not right. No wonder we are broke. This must stop. Do we have to go broke to protect our Country? If America ever wants to be free of these issues, then we need to quit giving them money. They are only laughing at us and our insecurity. We sent the Middle East 1.3 billion dollars, why? We should not have to give aid to prevent problems with other Countries.

Chapter 17...........Wasteful Spending

S ometimes scientists do need money for certain studies to further our future existence. Many diseases are harmful to us and the study to cure them is needed. However, the following expenses are just ridiculous.

We spend almost $200,000.00 on sex reversal in mice. Do we really need to know if we can change the sex of a male mouse to a female mouse? Why is this more important than our Social Security or our debt problem? We would not have such a debt problem if it weren't for the approval of such nonsense.

Then we spend over $220,000.00 on why men do not like condoms. Come on guys, is this really necessary to spend this kind of money on such of a thing. It really is common sense why a man does not like condoms. This is preposterous and makes me sick to think that this money is wasted on sex and condoms.

The University of Chicago is spending over $120,000.00 on how drugs are used for sexual enhancement. I'm sure grandma and grandpa would rather know the answer to that than get their pension check this month. Does Congress sit around and try to figure out what they can blow our money on?

How about almost $200,000.00 for the study of sex and the homeless man? Do we really give a damn how much sex a homeless man has or doesn't have? Actually, it's none of our damn business. Congress thinks it is their business.

This one will knock your socks off; we spend 2.6 million dollars teaching Chinese prostitutes how to drink. They had to dig really deep for this one. Can you believe this? We must put an end to this. We work way too hard for our tax dollars to be spent on this garbage.

We also spend over $200,000.00 for the study of the sex life of college freshman. Majority of college students have sex, so why is this so important? Maybe Congress has just figured out that they do have sex.

The study of sheep is costing us over $330,000.00. Can you believe this is almost a half million dollars? This is so incredible it's hard to imagine. We would like to have all the money divided between us tax payers that was used for these stupid studies. We would be in our glory to get ahead on our bills.

When it comes to our government, it seems there is always more and more money flying out the doors. We must pay more attention to what they are spending our taxes on.

Another study using almost $400,000.00 of our taxes is going for someone to cruise gay bars in Argentina for about 730 nights to determine why they enjoy sex after drinking. Here goes almost a half million dollars on some more stupid stuff. This is so remarkable I or anyone else would find this really hard to believe. If our President is allowing these kinds of expenses that are draining us to continue, we better consider impeaching Obama. Our Nation as we know it is in trouble and we can't let these expenses take us under.

The Virgin Islands is approximately 1,000 miles away from Miami, Florida. It's a place where maybe just a few Americans would visit a year. But Congress wants to spend 50 million dollars to support a park there, which will cost us over 1 million to maintain it. It is 2900 acres of land that we will never recoup that money or barely use. Why would we waste this money on land, which 99% of the population will never get to use or enjoy? Who are we doing this for and why are we going further in debt for a park out in nowhere land? This is another one of our government official's ideas that really takes the cake. Did you know that we spend tens of millions of dollars on parks? Please show us what is done to these parks to cost this kind of money. Something is awful fishy about this park thing.

There are many other studies that only use thousands of our dollars instead of millions. Gee, isn't that a sigh of relief? We spend almost $30,000.00 on the study of how methamphetamines affect the sex drive of a female rat. Then only about $10,000.00 on the sex drive of mice when they are deprived of food. The only rats we should be doing a study of, is all the rats we have in office right now.

The University of Syracuse spends thousands of dollars to study why college girls have sex after drinking alcohol. Can you believe that our tax dollars cover all this nonsense? Why it's so unbelievable that words can't describe it.

Did you know that the state of New Jersey pays 1 million dollars for every 1" of snow removed? Heh, all you guys with snowplows better move to New Jersey, you would make a killing. Just think a 6" snow storm would bring you 6 million dollars and you could retire. This can not possibly be true. If it is, then no wonder the United States is drowning in debt.

The Cash for Caulkers turned out to be quite the expense. It only cost $26,000.00 per home to caulk. Maybe we should become a caulker. It pays about $30.00 an hour. Can you even imagine this kind of expense for caulking? You can put 13 good size new windows in your home for about $13,000.00. Wouldn't it have been cheaper to do that? I bet Obama is having a blast just spending all our taxes on as much stuff as he can. He uses our taxes like it's his own bank account. He wishes.

The Van Couver Olympics was quite the conversation piece lately. I heard the health officials passed out 100, 000 condoms to all the athletes at the Olympics. Gee, who do you think paid for that? Why did these men need condoms, perhaps, to help prevent bruising from pole vaulting? Damn, just where are these athletes going to find the time or energy to indulge in sex while competing in the Olympics. And if they did, why are we paying for this nonsense. This is disgusting regardless of what the reasoning is.

There is about 4% of the United States population that does not have access to high speed internet. Can you believe that our government wants to spend 9 million dollars, to provide this service to the 4% not receiving this service? Here goes some more wasted money. Is it worth spending that kind of money on such a minority?

To encourage people to get involved with the 2010 census, our government spent one million dollars to stuff fortune cookies with a note saying "Put down your chop sticks and get involved in the 2010 census." Was this really needed? No one really wants to fill out the census because the government is to damn nosy. We can appreciate the fact that there needs to be a population count, however, why do they need to know how much we make and how we heat our house and many others questions that is none of their damn business.

In order for our census to be done, the government spent 5.6 million dollars to train census workers. It costs about 14.7 billion to do the census. It would have been much cheaper to hire our unemployed people and put them to work. It would have helped our citizens who need money and there would not have been as much spent looking for individuals for the position. Then the test on the computer was a 20 minute test and majority of the people could not finish it in 20 minutes so they were not eligible for the position. How much training is required to go door to door asking how many people live there or giving them a form to fill out? This process is much easier and cheaper to do than our government wants us to know about.

It is bad enough that for each answer we refuse to give, they want to fine us $100.00 per question. This is disgusting. We the people are getting really tired of being bullied and fined for such trivial things.

About 20 years ago, Congress spent 65 million dollars to develop an airplane, and to this day it can not get any higher than 2 feet off the ground. We might as well of ripped up that 65 million, because the airplane was just a waste of time and our money.

They have been working on a wind tunnel in Montana for a decade now, but gee people it has only cost us 70 million dollars so don't fret too much about this.

We could add all this wasteful spending to the book that is out there now, about all the outrageous spending the government has wasted our money on. It never ends. They blew another 50 million dollars on a rainforest project. I just don't see where this is helping our Nation. However, they only wasted 2 billion dollars on a highway in West Virginia that can not be used.

It's obvious that Congress is in need of help with the financial distribution of our tax dollars. How will we stop this? Someone must come forward and put an end to this insane spending.

For some reason the lawmakers are wondering what the outcome would be when monkeys smoke marijuana. The outcome was another $71,000.00 out of our tax money.

The only person that would blow this kind of money on things that won't help our Country is someone with an everlasting flow of money. Do you know who this could be? Well guess what? There is no one in this world that has that kind of money. So we have to stop all this pork spending. Obama is allowing it to happen and he must leave office as soon as possible. It is ridiculous how often he throws it in our face that he is the President. Believe this Obama, we know who you are, and we know that come 2012 you will no longer be leading our Country into the disastrous state that you have created now.

Then there is Florida that is receiving 3 to 5 million dollars to help the seniors from losing their medicare advantage. Why would this be happening? Perhaps our Health Care plan that Obama is cramming down our throats will help this out. By the sounds of it, not everyone will be covered, but of course no one wants to talk about what's in the bill till it's voted on. Has it ever made you wonder, if Obama even knows what's in the Health Care bill?

What about Conn. needing 100 million dollars for their medical centers? If a medical center needs that kind of money, perhaps they should hang it up. This is unbelievable.

In Lansing Michigan, they are getting $187,000.00 to protect the insect collections from being eaten by small insects. It sounds a little expensive to stop bugs from eating bugs. This is not going to help out our economy wasting money like this. Although I am sure art collections of any kind are important, I don't think they are more important than saving the Nation's economic crisis.

Back to the college girls, they are spending $219,000.00 on the pattern of how college girls indulge in sexual activity for a woman's health program. How damn stupid is this? Do we really need to know the pattern of their sexual drive or their pattern's for getting lucky? This money just flies out of Congress. This is almost to the point of being funny.

In Providence R.I. the police supervisors think they will do better if they get $95,000.00 to buy new blackberries for each supervisor. What did these cops do before blackberries came along? Years ago, the cops use to do a better job at protecting our streets than they do now, even without all this modern day technology.

I am sure you have heard about the $10,000.00 spent on 4 fish sculptures. Yes, you heard that right. Four salmon fish sculptures are costing that kind of money. Let's hope they are made of real gold or at least gold plated. It should bother everyone in this Nation to know where our money is going.

Good old Oklahoma is getting 1.8 million dollars to maintain some cruise boats to go down the Oklahoma River that has about a dozen passengers a day on a scheduled trip. I would think you could buy a couple new boats for that kind of money. We should wonder just what the hell our politicians are thinking. I do.

Here is another big waste of our tax payer dollars. The Mark Twain National Forrest is getting $460,000.00 to put in 22 concrete toilets in the middle of the woods. Who in the hell needs that luxury out in the boonies? There really has to be more going on than toilets out in the woods. What kind of toilets could possibly cost a half million dollars?

In Pasadena, California they are getting $259,000.00 to buy two bus wheeler polishers ordered from Australia. You mean to tell me that we don't build these here in the United States, which would be cheaper than importing them from another Country? This is just ridiculous how we spend and spend, when we can cut prices by shopping around and comparing costs.

When Obama signed our Stimulus Bill, it took place in a museum in Denver, Colorado and then Obama gave them a 2.6 million dollar grant. Why is it that Obama just offers to blow our money like it's in his own pocket? How will we ever recover from Obama's adventure in breaking our Nation?

At another University they are receiving $700,000.00 to create Robots that are funny or creative. This will really help out our situation. This is a crying shame. How can we laugh at a funny Robot when it's increasing our deficit or maybe that's supposed to help ease the pain?

Then there is one of our lovely states getting the sum of $325,000.00 for the study of how the environment affects the mating habits of a female Cactus Bug. Did you ever hear of such a stupid and wasteful event? Have you ever seen a Cactus Bug? Would you be more interested in its mating habits or seeing the prices of our food go down because we don't indulge in trivial issues like this?

A Los Angeles college is getting $327,000.00 to study some kind of sensory cell membrane in Zebra fish. How is this going to help our economy? It's time we admit to our selves that Obama is out to hurt us, instead of looking out for our best interest.

Dayton, Ohio is really trying to soar into the future. They are getting a half million dollars to put micro chips into their recycling bins, to track trash participation. What? Is this really necessary? No, it is quite the joke.

Leave it to the Feds for this one. A Federal building in Oregon is getting 133 million dollars to make their building more environmentally friendly. But one problem is that it will take 400 years to save that 133 million in energy cost. Can you imagine such a waste of money with no end result in sight?

We are spending $300,000.00 on a helicopter equipped to detect radio active rabbit droppings. Yes, you read it right. Gee, what else can we blow some of our tax dollars on? No words can express a quarter of a million dollars of our money going for this.

Then there is a company in Maryland that is getting $363,000.00 to tell all the stories about how the Stimulus

Bill created jobs. Please spare us the facts. There again, is more money going out for nonsense, then there is to create jobs. Let's face it, do you really know of any jobs that have been created on a long term basis? We are not talking about a bridge being built that will put guys to work for 2 months and then lay them off. What permanent jobs has Obama really created?

Washington has a Nuclear Waste Site that needs cleaned up. So they are getting 1.9 Billion dollars to get the job done. Of course it is going to create 2,000 jobs, until the job is done and then we will have 2,000 more on unemployment again. But again the jobs are not permanent. Why is it taking billions of dollars to clean up nuclear waste? Where did it come from? Why is it there? Why are us tax payers having to pay for this?

Louisiana has quite the crisis on their hands, they are receiving 60 million dollars to widen Interstate 10, and however, there is a big debate over replacing a bridge. Is it really needed? If they can't decide about the bridge, then why waste the money replacing it? How many kids, seniors and etc. could benefit from 60 million dollars?

In California, they are getting 54 million dollars to elevate and relocate about 3300 feet of a track for the Napa Valley Wine Train. Why does this have to come out of our tax dollars? Words seem to fail me when it comes to us paying this kind of money for this project.

We all remember the big switch from Analog to Digital right? For many of us we had to buy converter boxes for the transition. The government did give majority of us a coupon to reduce the cost of this box. However, were you aware that this major switch cost us 650 million dollars? Was this really necessary? This kind of money is a little bit much don't you think, especially when we are all hurting for money. We need to spend this kind of money on saving our Nation instead of updating our digital capabilities.

We should wonder why a restaurant in Missouri got $75,000 to renovate their space down town. Why did that come out of our tax dollars? I don't see the government giving any other business owners money for renovations.

Then there is a dinner cruise company that got 1 million dollars to put in a surveillance system to protect their vessels from terrorists. Why would Terrorists be a threat to a boat that served dinners? What a damn waste of more money.

This chapter should sicken the majority of people. Just to think of all this money being wasted on such ridiculous things when our economy is in such sad shape. Doesn't this just grind you to know about these expenses? What about all the expenses we don't know about? You know there out there. We the people could have used half of this money to lessen our debt, but no, we are not important enough. We need a leader that puts us and our Nation first.

In the state of Maine, they received a $30,000 grant to support the arts apprenticeship program for basket makers. If these basket makers can't weave our economy back into shape, then they should start making baskets at home using their own damn money.

What about a school in Massachusetts getting $150,000.00 to build a solar array on top of the school? Do you realize how many years it will take to get that cost back? What about all the other schools that are in financial trouble? They could use money like that to help with their problems. I guess it depends on who or what deals were made with Obama or Congress.

Then there is a Taxi Service that received $750,000.00 to maintain their taxies. Boy someone really cut a deal for that price. Why isn't the Taxi Company footing this bill?

North Carolina got $900,000.00 for a peanut company to produce and transport peanuts and peanut butter. That's almost a million dollars. Why so much? Makes you wonder.

There is a study done by Duke University that got a $500,000.00 grant for studying private issues on social networking sites like face book and etc. These sites do not need studying, they are open game, and if you're on there, then you are aware that there is no privacy. We fail to see the importance of this study.

A company in Arizona received $800,000.00 to put in light switches with motion sensors in them. Who the hell do they think they are that they need motion sensor light switches? This is a little much don't you think, especially when it's coming out of our pockets?

Allen Town, Pennsylvania was given $105,000.00 to repave, widen and stripe 14 miles of a bike trail. I guess they were trying to connect the trail in a park to another bike trail. Do we really need this kind of money spent on bike trails? When I use to ride a bike there were no damn trails. This is for very wealthy individuals and not something that should be coming out of our pay check.

California has 100 miles of flood control ditches with graffiti written all over it. So we gave them $837,000.00 to remove the graffiti. We all know once it is removed it will just be a matter of time before it looks the same as it does now. I know many people that would be glad to get rid of that graffiti for that kind of money. We might as well rip up one million dollars. It would have been cheaper to use our unemployed individuals or prisoners on a work program. Oops that was too easy to figure out.

Then there is the Shrimp Aqua Culture Research that got almost 3 million dollars. This is crazy. Why are we wasting money on this kind of research when we owe trillions of dollars? This is why we owe so much money because we are giving out too much money for things that are not important at this time. We need it all. We do not want to owe all this money just for someone to receive grants to continue their research. The only research that should be done is how the hell we are going to get out of this mess.

We must not forget the 2.5 million dollars for potato research. That sure would buy a lot of potatoes. What about the $206,000.00 being spent on wool research? That's crazy.

Not to mention the $200,000.00 spent on lobster research. A museum/library in Cedar Rapids received a half million dollars to put in more exhibits. It would have been fine with the exhibits that are there now. These items didn't even rate their own paragraph. Don't you just wonder what is wrong with our government that they approve all these expenses?

I would rather see the above 3 million go to help seniors buy their medication. Wouldn't you? This is all derived from ear marks or pork spending. These are the kind of items that are put into a bill that automatically get passed when the bill does get voted in. That's why pork spending has to be done away with. Obama said he would put a stop to pork spending, but he is guilty of continuing to sign the bills.

In Salt Lake City they have a foundation for an anti-steroid education program. They were given $250,000.00 for a foundation that states "I won't cheat". This is really bad; we are just wasting our tax dollars.

When it comes to bail outs we all know that they are breaking us in every way, shape and form. It is just a matter of time before the airlines want another bail out. This is getting ridiculous. Do you ever see the small businesses getting bail outs? They have to close down because that's their only choice. But these big company's seem to have a lot of guts asking for bail outs. The worse thing about it is that our government keeps giving these companies the money. The majority of them still end up down and out. It's just a vicious cycle and it hurts our pocket books.

The Department of Education is getting 100 billion dollars of Stimulus money after the teachers in Public Schools already received 23 billion dollars... The education lobbyists get a lot of this money, however, this is a lot of money, I find it very hard to understand why this much money is needed and would like to know just how it's being spent. It seems to me like there's a leech some where. Every school in the World should be able to run on 100 billion dollars. This is not right and we need to be more involved in how this Stimulus money is being spent.

Who paid for the security at Hillary's daughters wedding? We did.. Don't panic, it was only 5 million dollars. How ridiculous. Since when do we foot the bill for the Secretary of State's family functions?

But you know that's not as bad as Michelle Obama's trip to Spain for her vacation. She couldn't go on vacation with out her friends, so we paid for forty (40) of her friends to fly to Spain. They rented 30 rooms. Wow. The 757 jet they took cost us $11,351.00 per hour to fly there. The security alone to make sure nothing happened to her and her friends cost $75,000 a day. Yes, a day. Who the hell does she think she is? This is not right for us tax payers to have to pay this. And then try to explain to the senior citizens' why our Country is going broke and we have to cut Medicare. The fact that Michelle Obama will only wear designer clothing just makes me ill. So honey I hope your hubby can afford you after he is out of office.

The government continues to spend billions of dollars that we don't have. They are now robbing from Peter to pay Paul. The states need 180 billion to be bailed out. What in hell is going on? Since when does a state need bailed out? Evidently our Governors of these states are not doing their job or rather they are not doing a good job. For every state in need of bailout, the Governor from that state should be removed from office due to improper spending of funds. How simple is that? Then the Governor's would be more careful in their decision making when it comes to our money. Somehow, somewhere, somebody has to be responsible. Something must be done, we are at record deficits. It is a matter of time before the bottom drops out from under us.

Freddie Mac posts an 8 billion dollar loss and now they want 10.6 Billion more of aid to help them. Its time we let them resolve and go out of business. They are costing us too much money and they never seem to recover, they just keep going in the hole.

We keep sending money to these other Countries to help them, it's time Obama grew a backbone and said "No, we can no longer help you." Too many Nations are receiving funds from us while we are coming close to an economical meltdown.

What will these Unions that bleed us to death and these other Countries do when we are broke? I know, we will just print more money and become a poorer Nation. We won't have to spread the wealth; we'll have to beg the wealthy for help.

Gee, we are now spending millions of more dollars for Obama to go to India. This is such a waste of our tax dollars. Why would he go on an expensive trip like this when our economy is in such bad shape? This should prove to all of us that he is not interested in our state of well being. He would not be spending this kind of money if he were concerned for the United States. He is being greedy and does not care about cutting any cost to help us Americans. It appears that he is doing this on purpose to hurt us in some way. He definitely does not lead by example.

It was stated by a politician on TV that if we cut all earmark spending that we would not save any money. What? Who the hell are you kidding? If we cut out all earmark spending we would not have to worry about Social Security any more. The funds would be there. It disgusts me to hear these politicians try to manipulate us in to believing that. That's almost as bad as us needing to spend more money to get out of debt. Damn these people are idiots.

They want to spend 1.2 million dollars to convert an abandoned train station in New Jersey to a museum. We need money not museums.

Then there's the State University of New York who is spending $390,000.00 to study young adults who drink malt liquor and smoke marijuana. Who the hell cares about that? It does not warrant that kind of money coming out of our tax dollars to do a study on this.

We must not forget the $210,000.00 being spent in Hawaii to study the learning patterns of honey bees. As far as I know, we don't have this kind of money to be blowing on this either.

This is probably one of my favorites. They want to spend $554,763.00 to replace windows at a visitor center at Mount St. Helen in Washington State that's been closed since 2007 and the U.S. Forrest Service has no plans of reopening it. It just sends a chill down my spine to think that some idiot out there wants us to believe this is needed just so they can get more funds. I bet they don't replace any windows with that money.

Oh yes, lets spend $762,370.00 to study improved music in hopes to create satisfying works of art at Georgia Tech. To think that some professor desires this kind of money for his study while Americans are loosing their homes and going hungry, I don't think so chumps.

Our taxes are also funding a NPR Broadcasting channel on the radio and PBS channel on TV. Are you aware that our tax dollars are being spent on kid's shows with a big yellow bird? It was such a big shock to find out that my tax dollars are funding a children's show along with many others. This is not right. Again, what is wrong with our government that they continue to waste our money on garbage like this as opposed to concentrating on more valuable issues that need monetary attention?

The National Science Foundation has received over 3 million dollars to do research on teaching Robot's to fold clothes, how parents respond to trendy baby names, the impact on relationships by playing Farmville on Facebook, and the study of Shrimp exercising on a treadmill. The funding for these grants must stop. America is hurting and we must put an end to these ridiculous grants. Our hard earned money should not be wasted on such nonsense.

We also fund other stupid research programs such as Jello wrestling and if users of online dating sites are Racists. Americans you have no idea of what our taxes are being spent on. These are only a few of the thousands of grants that are breaking our Country.

Chapter 18 ....Expectations

We the people of the United States have high expectations of our government. We expect them to make logical decisions, defend our Country and promote growth. Some people are not interested in politics and could care less what is involved or who is doing it. Others want to participate in it, be an official or perhaps just follow the proceedings. It takes a special person to run for Presidency, or any office for that matter. For those that are in office or running for office, it takes a lot out of a person. The responsibility alone is a heavy burden. We the people elect an individual that we seem to respect and trust. However, majority of the time, that person turns out to do the opposite of what they said when campaigning for that position. Why is this? Why can't we rely on elected officials any more?

We are tired of hearing one thing and getting the other. They make promises and reassure us that they will be fighting for our wants and needs. Then before you know it, their in office and have been persuaded by another source to go against our every need. Is it the old timers in office that have been there way to long because we don't have term limits? Is it just plain out lies so they get elected into office? Well, we want to know what's going on. Why do we tolerate such acts? When you really think about it, once their in office there is nothing we can do to get them out until the next election.

So now that America is in trouble, we need to really pay attention to the people running for office. We know that we have to get the majority of Congress out of there. The responsibility of how our Country fairs will now be in our hands. We must make good righteous decisions. If there is any kind of Progressive, Radical, Marxism or Communist ways, about any person running we must choose not to vote for them? There are many good people out in this World that would do a much better job than what we have in office now.

It would be so nice if Americans could forget about politics and live our lives. But now the politicians have been so crooked, it has opened our eyes to our future. With out our participation, things could turn to a real disaster, very quickly and uncomfortably. I for one do not want to forge for food, worry about paying my heating bill, struggle to earn a dollar, and worry about not getting health care. We have it easy now compared to what it could be like if we don't change things ourselves. We must adapt and overcome as our government gets out of control.

As we live our every day normal life, as we may call it, it is nice to feel safe and not worry about war. It would be such a terrible thing to have to face. We trust our military and our brave soldiers to protect us and not let any harm come to us. We can wake up every morning and have no fear. We don't have to hear bombs going off or fires starting from the perils of war. We are safe and content knowing that our military has trained our soldiers to protect us. It is such a great feeling when you don't have to fear that today you could die from bombs or grenades. The blast alone would be terrifying.

This of course is a great expectation that the Whitehouse will keep us safe. But not only is there war to worry about, but now we have an embodiment of evil present in our Capital. Our very own President is bringing our Country harm. We must be more afraid of this than war. In war, you can win or loose, but there is an end. With Obama, spending his pants off with our money, there is no end. We will suffer for the rest of our lives. It is not necessary to spend like this. Who ever heard of spending your way out of debt? They must think we are stupid.

We need a new financial adviser, one that is capable of seeing our debt problem and is willing to stand up to Congress and say we don't have this kind of money to spend.

I am sure every one has heard of Glen Beck. I never miss his shows. He brings an insight to what is really going on. The great thing about it is, he is right in what he says and he is warning us to take control of our lives and save money, food, and other items to help us get through the hard times that could be coming our way due to government malfunctions. Well my dear fellow citizens, we must lower our expectations in our government and expect more out of ourselves. Being prepared will help any crisis.

The Tea Party Movement has realized that the problem in Congress is way out of control and what a better way to unite and organize by meeting and discussing issues, in hopes of being heard by our government. Have you noticed that the government is ignoring anyone that is against their opinions and rules? We don't like being ignored. It leads us to believe that all our thoughts of poor governing are true and they are blocking us out. Do you realize that only a few select people are chosen to sit in on Obama's speeches? They are the ones that think and believe like he does, so only those people are allowed in. That's what I call a very controlling government. They are scared to face those of us with opposing thoughts and strength to disagree with their future plans for our Nation. Obama tends to ignore a lot of situations that arise within our political system.

We as citizens have a lot of expectations from our government, after all they work for us and we pay them an awful lot of money to do their job. A fine example of the government not doing their job would be the crisis in Egypt. This is horrific. The chaos and protesting is way out of hand. These people are demanding that their government make some changes, because these people are out of food, water and worst of all patience. A big majority of them have no jobs, hence no money.

The rioting and looting has gotten so far out of control that it's just a matter of time before the military is called in to help. The citizens of Egypt are sick of being treated the way they have. The rebelling is so dangerous and scary that to watch this on TV just makes me speechless. Our reporters and camera men are being severely beaten and put into the hospital. Instead of these people wanting the World to know of their treatment, they are abusing and harming anyone and everyone in their path. They have become uncivil and demonic with rage.

What if we are next? Are we prepared to deal with this kind of disaster? No Country is prepared for retaliation from its citizens. This is what can happen when the people's priorities are not the same as the government's priorities. The government can not ignore the will of the people. This only causes problems as we can see. Although we as Americans would like to think we are above such dealings, I would tend to think that we are no different than those in Egypt. We must hope that our government is more concerned with our well being as opposed to the Egyptian government. Time will tell.

We pay our government well and expect an orderly Nation in return.

Chapter 19 ....New Laws

N ow that things are getting out of hand in Congress and the Whitehouse, it is time to implement new laws that should take effect by the next election in 2012. Obviously the laws regarding members in office are not working out real well in a Democratic society. So it is time for Congress to receive their new laws that are mandated by the people.

To start out with, the first new law should be; Congress can not vote on pay increases for themselves. How convenient for them. They will receive a pay increase by the cost of living allowance that is allocated. No more or no less. This is bound to save us lots of money, as long as their not voting for themselves to get a big raise.

Next, would be term limits. No elected official can be in office so many years that they can learn to abuse the system. We need a bigger turn over in Congress which would allow fresh blood and new ideas.

All elected officials loose all their benefits after their term is up in office. No more health care being paid for. No more extra's for them. They return to being a citizen with the same rights and rules as us.

Any funds in the Congressional Retirement Account will be transferred to Social Security. They then will collect Social Security like every one else. Any individual that is retired will no longer pay taxes of any kind, no property taxes, school taxes, FICA taxes or Federal taxes. If you have worked all your life, there is no reason you should have to pay taxes until you die. Of course there are special rulings for those who have not worked the majority of their life.

A good way to promote more education for boys getting out of high school would be to bring back the draft. It made men out of boys and a more secure Nation by having more trained men. There would be no draft for married men or men going to college. This would encourage men to either start a family or educate themselves for further development or train to become a soldier that loves his Country and wants to protect it. It would keep many idled teenagers off the streets and out of trouble. This is not the time to cut our military back by 25%, it is the time to reinforce our military to become a stronger Nation and remain that way.

It is time for our Department of Energy to get busy and lessen our dependency on Foreign Oil. If we can not do that, then the Department of Energy is not needed. One of the most important factors in our survival is energy. We must broaden our knowledge and strengthen our sources to continue to be a free Nation.

Global Warming has been questionable for many years. We have some of the smartest scientists in the World, so why can't it be decided whether or not there is, or is not, a threat of Global warming? If they can't decide, then let's get new people to work on the project. We need to know for a fact, before we waste any more money and time preparing for something that will never happen or perhaps something that we will never be able to fix. If Congress has such a compulsion to spend our money, then I think it would be better spent on scientific research that will give us an end result to help out mankind.

It seems all government agencies tend to fail more often than not. No more bail-outs for any company that the government has a vested interest in. Money that changes from one pocket to the other will never be a successful journey, we must let them fail. Bail-outs are the tax payer's dollars, and they must come to an end.

Any government run agency that needs help must be voted on by the people and not the government. There is a conflict of interest there and it must not happen. Look at several government run agencies. There is the post office that is barely staying above water, and then there is Social Security that the government has tapped into so much that it's broke. They must quit raiding the Social Security Funds. The government always wants to target the Social Security Funds first. Why is that? I maintain it is because there is so much money there that they can't keep their fingers off of it.

What about Fannie Mae and Freddy Mac financial institutions, they are drowning in debt and want more and more money from our taxes to stay afloat. With the government owning more and more auto manufacturers and banks, they are going to fail and want even more money to bail their ass out. No, we can no longer afford to bail out our government's mistakes because of their mass spending. Enough is enough.

Obama and his sidekicks will have to be put on a budget system, in order for America to remain free and strong. There must be a law stating that the President can not use an executive order to pass a bill that he can't get passed by Congress. That puts us Americans at risk and should not be allowed. The executive order is only to be used in case of an emergency that Congress fails to acknowledge, and it would harm America if the President did not use this executive order. Our Commander in Chief being Obama is abusing our system and our Constitutional rights. We must oppose his goals and plans for our Nation. If we don't, our future, our children's future and our grandchildren's future will no longer exist and we can **Kiss Freedom Goodbye**.

Another law that we will implement is, No more blackmail and bribes. How can our Country function to its highest potential when we have Congress and our President making deals and bribing people right in front of our face? There will be immediate jail time for any deal making. Congress better watch what they say and do or they will become a felon and out of a job. What kind of society is being created when you have leaders that we are supposed to trust, and then they turn on us or anyone who gets in their way. We will not stand for this.

We must admit to ourselves that taxes are necessary. However, we will lower taxes and put more money back into our pockets. An individual can not survive the tax hikes that Congress wants to push on us. Because of their evil spending we should not be punished. Soon it will not be worth working because there will not be anything in it for us. We do not want the government to take care of us; we just want to be left alone.

Property taxes will be lowered also. Why are we paying so much money to have a home? Many people could afford to live a better life if it weren't for all the taxes imposed upon us.

No more spending on Foreign Aid. If you are not American then you will receive no benefits of any kind. That means medical help and housing. We will not buy oil from the foreign Countries. We will no longer send money to other Countries for any reason. We help our own first. When we get out of debt then perhaps we will become more charitable.

Our military will be reinforced and become the strongest in the Universe. We will not sign any agreements that will not allow us to retaliate. This is America, the land of the bold and the brave. We will not take any thing from anyone, and in return we will not bother other Countries or become involved in their problems. As long as we are left alone to carry on with our lives, there is no reason to go to other Countries and fight for their problems. But remember this; do not step on our toes. As Americans, we will not tolerate any Terrorism or threats.

The most important new law will be No more foreign languages on any packaging we buy from the store. This is ridiculous. How many times have you tried to find the instructions for something in English? There are sometimes 3 or 4 different languages in the instructions. Damn It. This is America, why should I have to look for the English version. If foreigners want to live in America and be Americans then learn to read English. Why should we be put out to accommodate them? I once bought a DVD player; the instruction booklet was 100 pages long. After looking and finding the English part of the instructions it was only 25 pages long. What a waste of our money and time to help the foreigners be more comfortable in America. I will repeat that; AMERICA! I fail to understand why it has to come to this. It even bothers me more to make a phone call and hear; push 1 for English. What the hell is going on?

The next helpful law for many will be toward the Insurance Companies. When trying to purchase automobile insurance, what does your credit score have to do with your driving ability? Because a person has a bad credit rating their car insurance is higher. We must put a stop to this ruling. I fail to see the reasoning for this. Perhaps they think that if your credit is bad you won't pay your car insurance. Imagine that, they are not going to let us get away with out having car insurance so the jokes on us. How we drive and how we pay our bills is totally different and we should not tolerate being treated this way.

It seems Obama isn't doing a very good job on our illegal immigrant situation. It looks like Arizona has taken matters into their own hands and has made it illegal for illegals to come into their state. Good for them. Finally someone had the guts to do something about it. You see, Obama wants to give all illegal immigrants amnesty so they will be oh so happy with Obama and give him their vote for 2012. Isn't this ridiculous what our President will do to get a vote? We must not let this happen. Obama has done enough harm to our Nation, let alone giving him another four years. His term must come to an end, no matter what it takes for us to stop it.

Values and principals are important to us Americans. Unfortunately, Obama has different values and principals then we do, and that is just unconstitutional. Majority of us do not want to have illegals in our Country. They take away jobs that certain businesses would have to give to us, but because their illegal, the business cuts their pay and expects the same work, so it is cheaper for them. I can almost understand why the businesses are trying to cut costs; however, it should not be at the expense of our fellow Americans being employed. It all boils down to the neglect that the government is giving to our Nations businesses. They need help and support, but they just don't get it.

There is one law that is well needed, and that is Torte Reform. It is to limit the frivolous lawsuits that have been going on. We can only hope they enforce this law as much as possible. Remember the lawsuit with Mc Donald's and the hot cup of coffee? Well those are the kind of lawsuits that are trying to be prevented. It is pretty bad when Americans have resorted to suing someone for such trivial things. People seem to be looking for money in all the wrong places, and it makes me sick. When someone can sue you for something really stupid, then our society is going to hell. If you are one of these sue happy people, then you need to regroup and go to work for a living and quit trying to sue the pants off someone just to get a buck.

The Food Safety Modernization Act is going to be a real problem for Americans. This increases the power of the F.D.A. This will mean higher taxes for us and the price of food will go through the roof. They want to protect us from our food. How crazy does this sound? Soon they will be telling us how to grow our vegetable gardens and what animals can be near your gardens and how your soil has to be amended. We do not want any part of this kind of control. What the hell ever happened to growing a nice little garden for you and your family without having it inspected to see if you have done it their way? This is getting way out of hand and we need to put a stop to this ridiculous take over.

Chapter 20...................Do You Believe

After speaking to many individuals, their beliefs are of concern. Some people believe that our very own government had something to do with the 911 disaster. Do you believe that? I don't ever want to believe that is possible. That is absolutely terrifying to think that our government would purposely kill thousands of its own people. What would they accomplish by doing such a cruel thing? To this day, I will believe it was an act of Terrorism, and I hope every one will believe that also. If someone has any proof of this matter, they should come forward and let us Americans know about this inhumane act that was done to our fellow Americans.

I guess these people who blame the government are called 911 truthers. It amazes me how people think in our Country. We are very smart people and just because the government can't budget our money does not mean that they are willing to murder our own people. We should hope not any way. They are guilty of many things but not that. What if it were true? Why would they do that? What would they have to gain by that? That is a far off accusation, if you ask me.

Do you believe in our government? Do you believe they are corrupt? We have lots of proof of them being corrupt. They do it right in front of our face. You can hear them lying from one speech to another. I can't help but wonder, what they are thinking when they catch themselves saying one thing in one of their speeches and then contradicting themselves during another speech. This would seem pretty embarrassing, don't you think? Perhaps that is part of politics, you just laugh it off when you get caught lying and hope next time you speak you can amend the lie some way shape or form. Maybe lying is a prerequisite to run for office and then mandatory after you become elected. They surely must have schooling on how to deceive the people, lie and scam the public. They go to UDLS, the University of Deceit, Lies and Scandals. I believe it's only a two year term to receive your bachelors of assholes and a four year term to become a master bastard.

Do you believe that our America is safe and will never fail? Well think again, because we are definitely not safe. We will only fail because of the path our government leads us down. We want to believe that "all is well." It is only human to think for the best. This is America, how can it possibly be in danger from the people who we trust to run our Country? Our financial situation is about to destroy us. Let's hope we can save our Country before our freedom is lost forever.

We should fear our great leader Obama. He is in disguise. Do you believe he is pure and looking out for are best interest? Why is he shoving health care down our throats? He can not be trusted if he is defying our every desire. If the majority of the United States does not want this, then why is he pushing it on us? What does he get out of this? Wouldn't you think that he would want to appease us and not anger us?

What about the school district in Philadelphia? The teachers gave the students lap tops to take home; they were equipped with web cams, in the event that they were lost or stolen, they could find them. And to everyone's surprise, the Web Cams were activated; and pictures were taken of everything the students were doing. I'm sure that included dressing and undressing in their rooms. It is estimated that they took 56,000 pictures from the web cams. If there were that many pictures taken you know damn well they saw some things that they should not have. Talk about privacy being invaded. It is getting pretty bad when the schools are invading a students home life, even if it was an accident. This is not right. Someone predicted that some day our government would be watching us in our homes. I guess that idea isn't as far out as we thought.

Because the Unions are in bed with our lawmakers, it is really hard to fire someone who needs to be fired. It was refreshing to know that one of our state's schools fired all their teachers, approximately 74 of them. Do you believe they needed to clean house and the Union would not let them fire the teachers that were not doing a good job with their teaching techniques, so they fired all of the teachers. Now they can sort out the good and the bad and bring back the few that were good teachers. However, a new bit of news just stated that they have to call all the teachers back. Where is the justice here? It is a crying shame that others have to suffer because of our Unions. These Unions are a joke. All they want is to protect the bad teachers and collect Union dues from each person. Gee, how can they get rich without getting their dues? The best thing for our Nation is to get rid of the Unions. Obama spends too much time trying to patch things up with the labor leaders and kissing their back sides. The Unions are trouble and in order to gain control back we must rid our jobs of these Unions.

The Unions are getting so bad that Ford Motor Company built a plant in Brazil because the Unions would not cooperate with them. And what about Delta Airlines, they also are voting down the Unions. It's just a matter of time before other big corporations smarten up to their tactics.

Some of the happenings in Congress should make us feel like were watching Ripley's Believe It or Not. There is a meaning behind every award given. But one of the most outrageous, stupid, and ridiculous awards given, was giving President Obama the Nobel Peace Prize. What in hell did he ever do for us or our Nation to warrant him getting this? It is hard to believe that Obama would even accept this. We should hope he was embarrassed as hell to receive the Nobel Peace Prize. The good news is, some foreign Countries want Obama to give it back. Amen! For once I agree with them. He should have given it back as soon as it was presented to him.

His buddy Rev. Wright and Mr. Faircon must have been a little jealous of Obama receiving his Nobel Peace Prize, because they decided to present themselves with an award called The Living Legend Award. What a joke. Can you actually see these men accepting their own award? I do believe the three of them are a legend in their own minds. Awards are nice to receive when they have been earned. Any award earned is something to be proud of. Let's not take the meaning out of earning an award.

Obama has said that he will not raise taxes for anyone who makes less than $250,000.00 a year. Do you believe this? There is no way he can afford not to raise our taxes because of the outrageous spending he is doing. You watch, soon he will be saying he has to raise our taxes due to the economy crisis that he put us in. How could a man with such lying abilities get elected into office?

This should not come as a surprise to you, considering who is in charge of these stupid new laws. But since when do we use the illegal workers as rats? They are ratting out the companies they work for. If an illegal is employed by a company and he or she does not get the same amount of pay or hours as the other employees, then the illegal employee has a right to turn their boss in for breaking wage and hour laws. By turning their employer in, they are told they won't be deported. Have you ever heard of such a joke?

These are illegal's we are talking about, they shouldn't even be in our Country, and now they have the right to turn in a business. Wow, do you believe this; this world is going to hell. Our labor laws should not pertain to an illegal. They are not citizens.

They are now considering a New School Pay Plan sort of like a teacher's bonus program. If the children succeed the teacher will get a bonus for good teaching. Please tell me this is not true. They get paid to teach. But because the schools are doing so poorly, they want to give some incentives to the teachers. Their damn paycheck ought to be their incentive. Guess who will be paying for this before it's all over with? Of course this will be us, you and me. What is going to stop the teachers from cheating and changing test scores just so they get their bonus?

Do you believe they want to make Puerto Rico a state? They do not want to become a state. They are being tricked into becoming a state by our government. Obama figures that if can make Puerto Rico a part of the United States than he will have a better chance of winning the 2012 election. He is hoping for their vote. As bad as our economy is now and he wants to bring forth another state for us to be responsible for. Obama does not make any sense in his decision making. He is only concerned with what will benefit him and to hell with us Americans. As you know, this will add more money for us tax payers because of the Health Care Bill. Now we will have to give them Health Care also, which we can not afford.

Do you realize that they hid the expense of the Health Care program until after the voting was done? Because it was going to cost us a lot more than they predicted, they did not want to bring it up before the vote or they

151

might have turned the vote down. It really should become null and void now because the numbers were held back on purpose, that is basically tampering with the votes. Obama and his sidekicks sure know how to hide things. This is not acceptable to us. We demand that another vote be done, now that we know this Health Care is going to put us deeper in debt. We must repeal this Health Care Plan and focus on bettering our insurance programs that we have now, such as Medicare.

After seeing all the crooked events taking place on Capital Hill, it appears that we should elect an individual that over sees all the actions that take place in our Congress. Someone who will not let any kind of misdealings take place. We need someone who does not have power over the President, but will be like a watch dog to prevent all the corruptness. This person is needed and should be considered. The first time this person holds back any shady deals, then he will be fired. Americans we need to do something to prevent all this madness that is taking place in our government.

One event that has taken place and shown us that we can no longer trust our government to back our Nation; is those students in California being punished for wearing T-shirts with the American Flag. Since when is it illegal or a crime to honor our Nation by displaying the flag on a shirt? This is unforgivable; we can not allow things like this to happen to our society. The school stated that it was insensitive to the Mexican students. Well who cares! This is America and by wearing its colors should be an honor and not a crime. It should actually inspire the Mexicans to become an American and not offend them. California is really starting to separate its self from the other states. It comes up with the stupidest ideas. Gee I wonder if Pelosi had any thing to do with this. Somebody somewhere is becoming a traitor.

Here is a fact that will curl your hair; Ms. Pelosi has her own personal jet that we Americans pay for. But the shocking part of all this is, our taxes pay for her liquor cabinet to be stocked inside the jet. It only cost us $100,000.00 a year, gee that would pay off the majority of an individuals bills for the whole year, and this is just for her booze habits and entertainment aboard her jet. Gee I wonder if she belongs to the mile high club. These kinds of expenses tend to really get our goat. We know our government officials make enough money to furnish their own damn booze.

Times sure are changing for us Americans. It is almost as if we are in a new Country. I cannot believe what I am hearing about all the new rules and laws that are taking place in our states.

A health official in Massachusetts is passing out condoms to children as young as three years old. Now please someone somewhere give me a reason that would convince me that this is okay. What does a toddler know about sex; let alone what to use a condom for. Who is the sick mother _____ that has Okayed such a thing? We better pay a little more attention to the people running our schools. If something is not done soon, you will see your eleven year old having sex on your couch thinking its okay.

Then to top it all off we are letting ten year old children use firearms to hunt. I refuse to think that someone out there is dumb enough to put a gun in a child's hand. The mental capacity of a ten year old is very immature and they barely know how to use good hygiene let alone fire a gun. Ask yourself this question; would you go in the woods to hunt if you knew there were five, ten year olds out there with .30-.30 rifles shooting at what may be a deer? If you said yes, then you're as crazy as our government. This nonsense has to stop. We must let children be children before they leap into killing something with a gun. They will grow up with no empathy or any morals. In another twenty years these same children with a condom in their pocket and a rifle over their shoulder will be the next generation of serial killers.

Whose idea is it to consider a proposal to build a Mosque near ground Zero? You would have to be a complete idiot to expect us as Americans to accept this building. These people use our planes to kill our people and destroy our property and we are going to allow them to build near the area they did all this. This is a joke, I can hear them laughing at us right now. Is this a test for the Americans to see just how far they can push us? It's even worse to think that we are going to allow this to happen. Who the hell is paying for this? We want to know? Who ever it is, it better not be an American. Turning the other cheek is one thing but stabbing us continuously while we watch is another.

Every year on 9/11 we display the name of every person killed from those planes hitting the Twin Towers, if we could ask each one of those people what they thought of this idea, it would cause a major earthquake from all of them rolling over in their graves from disgust and shock of even the thought of such an idea.

Thanks to Obama, no one has received a cost of living raise in two years. He says there has been no inflation and therefore there should not be a cost of living raise. My dear Americans, you have had to experience the drastic increase in the prices of things lately. Why does Obama lie to us like this? How stupid does he think we are? The price of gas alone has gone up at least 20 cents in the last few weeks, not to mention how much more our groceries are costing us. Just recently, I heard on TV that soon the prices will be so outrageous that no one will be able to buy anything. They are talking $77.00 for a can of coffee, $42.00 for a carton of orange juice, $15.00 for a chocolate candy bar and $45.00 for a box of sugar. Can we really afford this? We will all go hungry. There is no way anyone will be able to buy food. This is caused by the government spending so much money and having to print more and decreasing the power of our dollar. This is a joke.

We can not allow our government to do this to us. Now that the November 2010 election is over and many Republicans have taken over a majority of seats, at least there will be checks and balances now. This will help control Obama's bad habits, but I fear it won't be good enough until we get Obama out of office. Again Americans, you do know we have to vote a better Commander in Chief into office or we can hang it up.

It will take more time than we hope for us to straighten this mess out. But it would be nice to see a light at the end of the tunnel as opposed to pure darkness. Our future depends on our decisions and we must make the right decisions if we want to look forward to some kind of comfortable life style.

Can you believe that someone in Congress is or has considered using the law of the Islam here in our states? Are you aware what that is and how it could effect you?

Sharia is the law of Islam and the Muslims feel that we should practice this law here in our States. This would give them the right to kill their wife or children if they don't do as they are told or if they cheat on their husbands. Women aren't allowed to walk down the street alone or she will be arrested or stoned. They have no respect for women and treat them like dogs.

This is a law in their Country that they are very adamant about. We need to beware because there is a Judge in Florida considering this law. How un-American is this? This Judge must be stopped from making a decision like this. This is America and how dare they even suggest that we abide by this law. These people must be nuts. We do not need foreigners coming into our Country trying to tell us how to run our Country. If they don't like America the way it is then get the hell out. It should bother us to no end that these people are trying to throw their weight around and convince our government of such nonsense. Obama seems to favor the Muslim's and that is not good. Although this is a sticky subject we should keep any eye on Obama and his Muslim ways.

Why have we sent over 822 million dollars to the countries in the Middle East? This is astronomical. These people have the audacity to come forward and ask us for more. When you take into consideration that Quddafi is a Terrorist and we are giving our hard earned tax dollars to these kind of people, what possible explanation could there be? This kind of behavior tends to cause resentment from us Americans. This is madness.

Why is it that before Obama took office we barely knew much about the Muslim's and now that's all we hear about? For example; there is a Muslim school teacher here in our Nation that is demanding three weeks vacation after only one year of being employed so that she can participate in the pilgrimage walk to Mecca, this is a religious belief that Muslim's have and they must participate in this walk at least once in their life time. This is fine and dandy for them, but since when does it involve us here in our Country? The outrageous part of this whole thing is that our Department of Justice is suing the school for denying her this vacation. This is crazy; who the hell's side is our Justice system on? This should be of the utmost concern to us Americans. As stated above, why is every thing in our Nation now about the Muslim's rights? Could our very own President be a closet Muslim? We should consider this as a possibility and be on guard for his future plans with the Muslim's.

As we all know the election in November 2010 was quite the ordeal. The Republicans and Democrats were fighting for positions in the Senate and House. Due to the poor decision making on the Democrat side, the Republicans managed to take many seats away from the Democrats. Regardless of how hard the Democrats cheated at the polls and even rigged some of the voting machines, they still lost power. Due to this huge loss, the democrats were mentally burdened by such a loss. Because of their mental state, Congress called in grief counselors to counsel them through their trying times.

Yes Americans, do you believe this? Our tax dollars are being spent on these lying, cheating babies to bring up their spirits from such a loss. I can not imagine this being allowed to happen. If they took it that hard that they lost, then let them pay for their own damn shrinks and leave our money alone. Anyone who rigs voting machines and cheats and steals votes and still loses is quite the character, we do not want in Congress. Ha-Ha, you jerks. You deserve everything you get. Especially because you voted on issues that you didn't even bother to read. I wonder how many of our dear Democratic members had to be put on medication due to the nature of their loss.

What's the deal with parts of California banning pets? How cruel this comes across. It has been proven that pets can be very therapeutic for an individual and now they want to ban them. This doesn't make any sense. If they are having problems with pets then resolve them, but don't ban such a wonderful part of a person's life. Many people count on their pet for company; pets are loved like a family member. We should ban Congress from making any more decisions before banning pets. This is really hard to believe.

You're not going to want to believe this next sentence either. Did you know we dropped off 175 pallets full of 100 dollar bills overseas? We just passed it out like it was candy. Talk about wasteful spending. Just who decided on this cute little expense? This is amazing. We just can't stop these jerks from blowing our money. We can no longer afford to help these other Nations and yet Obama keeps tossing them more money. We are talking about billions of dollar's here. I am at a loss for words.

We as Americans know how the illegal immigrant situation is a problem. Some people could care less if their here in the United States or not. However, majority of us do not want them in our Country. It costs us way too much money to support them. Not to mention that by them coming here, they are taking away jobs from us. But the real kicker is the Dream Act. Are you aware of this act? It was going to cost us billions of dollars that we do not have. Congress wants to pay illegals to go to college or the military. This will allow them and their immediate family to become a U.S. Citizen. Can you believe this? We have so many Americans that would love to go to college to further their careers and better themselves and yet they want to help the illegals before they help our own citizens. What is wrong with our government? They have their damn heads screwed on backwards. Fortunately for us the bill did not go through. This is very unsettling to think that our government is willing to help out everyone else but us.

I still maintain that someone somewhere is not on the United States side. Too many things are happening and too much money is being distributed to other Countries that should not be. This is another reason we must clean out the Whitehouse and Capital Hill and start over with new blood.

Another one of my favorites is; why are prisoners receiving tax refund checks? Hello. What is going on, over 130 million dollars is going out to prisoners that don't have a job? We all make errors but this is too big of a problem just to be an error. This sounds a little fishy to me. We all need to take note of these mishaps and money that is floating around for miscellaneous nothings.

The other day I was in line at the grocery store and the lady in front of me was paying for her groceries with a bridge card (food stamps) that was fine until the cashier asked her for some money to pay for the toilet paper. Do you believe that she bought four bottles of pop which was covered under the food stamps but the toilet paper was not? What kind of garbage is this? Toilet paper is not a luxury like soda pop, nothing can replace it, and it was not covered by her food stamps. This is ridiculous, someone better look into this program and get a grip on what luxuries are and what necessities are. This just amazes me how messed up our government and their policies are.

I'm sure every one is aware of the shooting in Tucson, Arizona by a young man that is possibly mentally challenged. What a disaster. This probably wouldn't be as big of a deal, accept that there were politicians involved and in the hospital fighting for their life. Ms. Gifford is still struggling with her recovery. The Doctors don't seem to think that she will make a full recovery. We must pray that their wrong.

This young man who decided to get a gun and shoot all these people must be a real looser. He must have some real deep down problems that would cause him to want to kill people. At this point in time, I think they are still trying to decide if he knew right from wrong and if he has mental problems. Let's face it; anyone who would start shooting into a crowd of people can't be wrapped too tight.

The individuals with the real mental problems are those who accused Sarah Palin of being involved in this. Why would it be her fault? Why are so many politicians afraid of Ms. Palin that they have to bring up her name in hopes of demeaning her? She is one of the few politicians out there that minds her own business and doesn't pass blame on anyone. We need to fear the people who made these accusations. They are sneaky and should be looked upon as dangerous to our society. They want to start trouble and we don't need any more trouble. This is really hard to believe. It makes me speechless. They need to wear tinfoil on their heads, so we know who they are.

The next unbelievable event is that the Unions are trying to stop the Girl Scout Troops from selling cookies at the grocery stores. This just makes my head shake in awe. What in the hell is going on? Since when does our government side with the Unions and bust kids with lemonade stands and Girl Scouts from selling cookies? I don't like this. It's just one more step in the direction of controlling our every move. Soon there will be people from the Internal Revenue Service showing up at our yard sales with their hands out wanting a cut of everything you make. It's time Americans, to put our foot down and stop being a push over. We deserve better, we are better and we need to be treated better.

Can you believe your eyes when it comes to the issues in Wisconsin, what is going on? The Democrats have left town to avoid voting on a bill, while the governor of Wisconsin is awaiting their votes. This is against the law. We must hope and demand that something is done about these Democrats leaving and refusing to do their job. Who do they think they are that they can manipulate the system to their liking? It is mandatory that they loose pay and possibly be removed from their positions. They are using excuses such as; they don't have enough time to read it and other excuses that are unacceptable.

The real truth about the matter is they don't want to vote on these issues that deal with the Unions because the Unions and the Democrats are in bed together, so it's hard to get one of the Democrats to go against the Unions let alone all of them. They do not want to vote. This is part of their elected job and by refusing to come back and vote should be grounds for dismissal. To top it all off, our government is sending protesters to Wisconsin by the bus full to help protest. Since when does our government get involved in protests? It is so easy to see what is going on in our Country and who is behind the enemy lines. Even if our leaders are for the protesting of union leadership, it is important that they do not show it. The Unions are getting a little bit too big for their britches because they are now threatening the Businesses in Wisconsin with letters stating that they will be boycotted if they don't stand behind the unions. This is the kind of crime we do not need or want.

This is the first time in government history that so many elected officials have went against all the rules and are getting away with it. If Obama wasn't President they would not be getting away with such behavior. If something isn't done about these officials leaving town and refusing to vote, then it is just a matter of time before anyone in office can get away with anything they so choose.

What about the protestors that was present and was in need of a Doctor's excuse for missing work? How convenient for them that there was Doctor's there that were willing to pass out sick notes. Well how illegal is this? Why aren't they arresting these Doctor's for doing illegal actions? Have you noticed that the only time laws are enforced is when a citizen is involved, but yet no enforcing the law for the politicians or the crooks?

What is our World coming to when it comes to our children's education? Take Detroit, Michigan for an example. Do you believe that 42% of the students don't graduate? That says something about our school system and the Board of Education. What is going on? Why aren't more children graduating? Sounds like the teachers need more pep in their step. These kids should be graduating and going on to college. This is pathetic. The Detroit schools have about 81% of their students qualifying for the free lunch programs. Wow this isn't very encouraging for the future of many more kids to come. Sounds like Detroit could use a bail-out themselves. I think we need to be a little harsher on the kids and even more so on the teachers. With percentages like this, we can expect problems down the road. This isn't the only school in the United States that is having problems with children receiving a good education.

The schools now a days lack power to discipline. That is one of the problems. It's not so much what their taught, but how much discipline is enforced. For some reason the schools have lost the power to make these kids mind. It has been taken away from them because of certain parent's not wanting the school to have discipline power. It is hard to understand why a parent would frown on the school system for encouraging good behavior even if it meant punishing them for bad behavior. I can't believe how many parents' go "ga ga "over their kids. They seem to think that their precious ones are above being a bad boy or girl. Okay Mom & Dad what makes you think your kid won't act out? Especially when they are away from home and know that the school has no say in what they do or how they act. As far as I am concerned all children need discipline, some more than others. If we want better education, then we need to bring discipline back into the schools. Children need to know that there are consequences for bad behavior and therefore they will be more apt to be good and pay more attention and even learn something. Parent's need to quit making sissy's out of their kids. What the hell kind of World will there be in the future if children don't encounter some hard knocks along the way. They need to loose at games, they need to fall down and get hurt, they need to know that No is No! Strength will make them a better person and a responsible adult.

To give some examples of the government controlling us would be to look at all the VA hospitals. Are you aware that Obama will only allow four channels to be viewed on their TV's? The only news channel that he will allow is CNN. Why is this? What is he afraid of? There is nothing wrong with CNN, however, they do not go into detail or explain a lot of the news that is taking place. Obama will not allow Fox News to be turned on; it would have to be, because they are very thorough and tell everything that we Americans need to know. Our government does not want us to know about a lot of things and therefore they are controlling what they want us to hear. This is not right. I truly think something needs to be done about this. The audacity of Obama to control what we hear is very over whelming. It's just a matter of time before they limit what we watch. I am telling you, they are doing a lot behind our backs, if you only knew, you would be very angry.

We all should be concerned about the death of Usama Bin Laden. It is fantastic that he is no longer available to bring harm to our Country. But I am concerned about the way our government has handled this situation. Why has his body been disposed of so quickly? Why haven't they kept him around for a few days, so that there was verification by many of us Americans that this man is dead? Something is not right about his death. Now we must wonder if he really is dead, what the government is hiding and who is responsible for the quick disposal of his body? There is just too many loose ends here that I feel are a little wishy washy. I prefer to be wrong about this, but later on down the road, I feel there will be some kind of problem with this whole issue.

We need to thank our soldiers for a great job well done. It is wonderful to know that our soldiers are taking care of us and our Country. We must remember, who deserves the credit for the death of this Terrorist, because our soldiers deserve a big pat on the back for this one. I truly hope that Americans don't think Obama deserves the credit, because he does not! We must give credit to who really deserves it, and that of course is our Military.

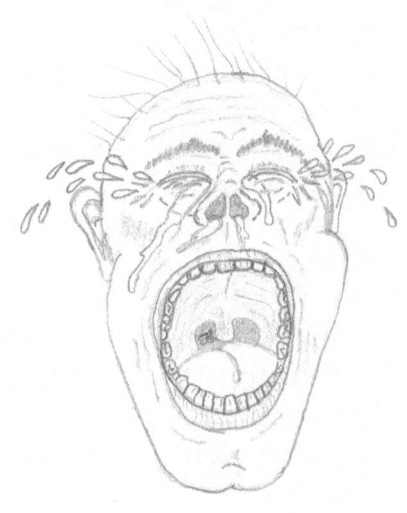

Chapter 21 ....Bad News

May I have your attention Americans? For those of you who have read this book and have gotten to this chapter, every page has been bad news. This chapter will cover some bad news that perhaps never crossed your mind. Now it's time to add two and two together. Unlike Congress, we will get four as the answer.

What is wrong with our Congressional Budget Office? How many times will they be bribed or bought to change the figures to accommodate Obama's desires? I am sure you have noticed with the Health Care Bill. One minute they stated it was not possible to do and after a meeting with Obama, then they found the funds available to accommodate the new bill. Do you suppose Obama gave them a bunch of money? No of course not, just some more behind the door secret deals. These back door approaches are really going to hurt America, if it hasn't already. Every time Congress thinks, they weaken our Nation. Because of all the secret deals and wasteful spending, we are not considered the top Nation as we once were. Surprise, would you like to guess who the top Nation is? It is China. This is very disheartening to hear. When America has been a strong Nation for centuries and now China has passed us up.

Speaking of China, The President of China has come to the Whitehouse for dinner. As we role out the red carpet he strolls down it like a king of the world. Obama and he will be having dinner and conversation. The worrisome part of all this is, the President of China is questioning the role of the United States dollar. He also stated that our currency system is the product of the past. Who his he to say this? Oh yes, he is our landlord. Gee we only owe our whole Country to him, I wonder why he is concerned? It is just a matter of time before he demands back the money we owe.

With all this being said, we must wonder what the hell is wrong with Congress that they want to raise our debt ceiling. How Funny. This is a joke. They want higher credit to waste more money. Americans it's time to start laughing at the idiots on Capital Hill. It's like a zoo. We need to turn Capital Hill into a petting zoo. We could walk by them and look at how stupid they look and act and maybe throw them a peanut or two. Best of all, just having them eat out of our hands would be a pleasure for the American people.

It is no wonder China has passed us up, if you stop and think about their education programs as compared to ours. Their children go to school twice as long as our children do, so they are bound to learn more and be smarter. Although we don't want our children to have to spend their whole life in school, it wouldn't hurt to ad on an hour or so. This would help in better educating them.

Unlike America, they manufacture more goods than we do at a cheaper cost. We are actually loosing businesses to China. It has been brought to our attention that there are people who actually are Americans but live in China and teach other American businesses how to move to China and become successful. This sounds like traitors to me.

When you really stop to think about how the Chinese live, it is a style of living that we as Americans do not want any part of. Many Chinese are unhappy and they have a higher suicide rate than America because of how they are treated by their leaders. They have no freedom and are worked to the bone. There is reason to believe that our leaders want us to go global so we will have to live like the Chinese. Believe me, you don't want that.

China has become more innovative than America but only because of the abusive treatment to their citizens. They are driven hard and put away wet, if you know what I mean.

What ever happened to individuals like Thomas Edison, the Wright Brothers and Ben Franklin? Americans are no longer thinking into the future anymore, we have become set in our ways and feel comfortable with what we have instead of trying to improve technology and better that of which we have. At this rate our society will diminish, we need to improve our desires for success.

China already has the fastest computer in the world and has become the home of the world's largest Solar Research Facility. Why don't we have it? Why isn't someone in America trying to top this? We thought we were pretty sassy with our jet stealth, but now China and Russia have one, and it looks very familiar, "Hmmm." Other Nations are passing us up and the whole reason this is happening is because of our government stunting our success by over taxing us and putting too many rules and regulations on businesses and individuals with good ideas and intentions.

Our government has seized our drilling for oil while China continues to buy as many oil fields as they can. Now China receives the better grade of oil and their refining costs are less because they get the purest oil. It costs us more to refine our oil because we now get the lower grade of oil which causes our gas prices to go up. If we were drilling for our own oil like we should be, this would not be a problem.

China looks more into the future for bettering their Nation and America sits idle while our government spends billions of dollars on garbage.

We must change our attitude toward the future of our Nation. However, this can not be done with out the assistance of our government and it seems they are more interested in luxury vacations and larger pay checks than they are with the future of America. Our government is creating lazy Americans by limiting our means and creating a nanny state.

"Necessity is the mother of invention" so we must not feel like we are in need of too much or we would be inventing more things. I feel that the government is too greedy to allow us to improve and become a stronger Nation. They want us weak and in need of their help.

Many Countries governments are failing. This is kind of strange, why all of the sudden are so many Countries in trouble? It looks like it's a plan; someone is forcing this to happen. I wouldn't be surprised if it has something to do with Global Government that Obama keeps speaking about. When you really think about it, we sure have become helpless by not being able to count on our government. This is why it is so important for each and every one of us to pay more attention to the individuals who are running for office. I still maintain we are better off to base our vote on someone who has high morals, is of good character, honest and has the desire to better America.

When Obama was a Senator, are you aware that he did not honor the American flag? Him and Michelle actually attended flag burning ceremonies. Please tell me why we never heard about this before he ran for President. He should not have been allowed to run let alone be our Commander in Chief. Obama doesn't even follow protocol when the National Anthem is played. This is disgusting to think that the man in charge of our Country does not appreciate our flag or our National Anthem. Something is very wrong here. Obama even spoke of disarming America to the level of acceptance to the Middle East. This is crazy. Why is our President defending and sticking up for other Countries?

My dear Americans we have a lot to fear because too many things are being hidden from us. Obama once stated that "when he becomes President he will put his hatred aside and use his power to bring change to our Nation." He states that the change is about to overwhelm the United States of America.

Well Americans, have you had enough? I sure have. The sorriest thing we ever did was to put this man in office. What bothers me the most is; this is the first black family that has ever taken office and he and Michelle have ruined it for other black Americans. He has proved to us that he does not know how to run our Country. The real tear jerker is that he doesn't seem to care.

Some real great news is that two of our ex Presidents raised almost 53 million dollars to send to Haiti to help. This was Bush and Clinton. What a great job guys, except no one has followed up on this money. No one knows what it was spent on or what was done with it. Wow, this is terrible. Either Bush or Clinton should have controlled this money to some degree to make sure it went for the proper items to help the people in Haiti. This is a lot of money. Perhaps we should do more fund raisers to help us get out of debt. It sure couldn't hurt.

Are you aware that the interest alone on America's debt is 4 billion dollars a day? Now just how in the hell are we supposed to repay this? The government is living beyond their means and someone needs to take their spending rights away. The only thing I can say is "Let me in there, I will show them how to cut costs". They just don't want to cut costs because it will deny them the luxurious life that they have been living.

The National Debt is about 14 trillion dollars right now, and we have spent one trillion in the last seven months. Congress you need horse whipped. We need a Congress that is accountable. We definitely know that the Congress we all know and love is not capable of being accountable. Damn.. I don't think their capable of running our Country or things would be better.

Do you realize that when Obama was a Senator in 2006 he voted against raising the debt ceiling? Now he is the President and he wants to raise the debt ceiling. He sounds a little fickle to me and he's not even a blonde. He claims we can't pay our bills if they don't raise it. Maybe Obama should get a second job to help pay for this mess he's gotten us into.

In his State of the Union Speech, every other word was to fund something or to invest in something. Gee Americans he can't even pay our Nations bills and he speaks of more investing and funding. This man has some kind of problem. He makes things sound good and simple, but it's not. It's expensive and he knows it, yet he speaks as if we have trillions to blow. Although his speech was exceptionally good, we must read between the lines. We must not trust his words just because he sounds convincing and comes across like he is concerned. This is just a ploy. After all what else can he really say to us? He is going to say what he thinks we want to hear. Please Americans, do not trust the words that come out of this man's mouth. Our National debt is the greatest threat to our American Security. The government is manipulating us into thinking that every thing is okay. As for those Americans who have been paying attention to our Nation's issues, well we know better.

It should worry us even more to know that he wants about one million electric cars on the road in the next 3 or 4 years. Who is going to pay for this expense? And if we have the funding for that, how many Americans can afford to buy an electric vehicle? To top it all off, these electric vehicles are not a good thing. The government is trying to go green and cut energy costs and now they want us to plug in our car and use more electricity to charge them up. Who is going to be happy about replacing the batteries in one of these cars when they go dead? Also on a long trip, just where are you going to charge your car? This would require charging stations all over the Nation. Sounds like more of our tax payer's dollars going astray. Going green will cost us more money and is a waste of time. It will only put us further in debt and do very little to help out with pollution. This green energy idea won't create jobs either. Another flop with the green energy idea is the new light bulbs. They have stated that they do not last as long, are bad for our eyes and they are not as bright. So what good are they?

Obama wants to out build the rest of the World. Here he goes again, more money that we don't have. America can't you see what he is doing to our Country? If you choose to elect this man back into office in 2012, you all need your heads examined.

Obama has leaked out information to Russia about Britain's submarine fleet and some of their top secret nuclear weapons right down to serial numbers. Britain is our friend; just why in hell would he do this? We must ask ourselves just what Obama has to gain by his actions? This isn't just scary, it's almost treason like. If someone could give us a real good reason for what he has done we would love to hear it. He sure is putting us on the spot with many other Nations. We need Britain as our friend. Damn it Obama, clean up your act. Our government is treating the Middle East better than we are treating our allies. Look at Israel, they also are an ally, but Obama is attempting to mess that relationship up also. Obama wants them to go back to 1967, the way the borders once were. That will hurt Israel very badly.

This would give part of Israel back to Palestine, and leave Israel with practically no land at all. What gives Obama the right to suggest that Israel give up their land? The only reason possible for this suggestion would be to help out the Muslim Countries. Obama is going to turn all our allies against us.

We must let Britain and Israel know that they need to be patient with us and forgive our President for his ignorance. The American people made a mistake putting Obama into office and soon we will try to resolve this problem come election time. When the meeting of the minds takes place at the United Nations, all the Countries get a chance to vote on certain resolutions. It is always the Middle East that votes against our Nation. So why are we treating them better than our allies?

Do you realize that other Countries owed us 23 billion dollars and Obama wrote it off? What? We wrote off a debt that we could have collected on and helped out with our debt problem and it basically has been forgiven. Do you think China would ever tell us, "Heh you guys don't worry about the trillions you owe us, just forget about it?" This is unforgivable. We must refuse to accept this. If we are owed money, this is not the time to forgive and forget. Too many more stupid acts like that will put us under.

Do you realize that over 75% of the states in the United Sates is about to go bankrupt? These states are in trouble, they do not have the funds to keep operating. So what happens next? We can't bail out each and every state. What is the next step? To watch our Country go down the drain is mentally draining to each and every citizen. Where does it stop? Who can stop it? This whole damn mess is scary. And the worst part about it all is we can't even count on our leaders to solve these problems.

Americans we are in such turmoil that something disastrous is bound to happen sooner than we think. The people who will be hurt the most is US!

Many of the other Countries like China, Russia and the Middle East have already gotten together and had meetings about changing the currency so that the American dollar is worthless. What Then? I am sure you have heard many say "Buy Gold" it will always be worth something. How many people can afford to buy gold and still maintain their monthly bills? Not many. In the state of Utah you can actually pay your taxes now with gold. It seems like we are regressing back to the old days.

That is why when we go down; the only people who will survive the crisis will be the rich. They can turn their dollars into gold because they can afford to. The majority of the rich in this Country are socialist, and we really do not want any part of that. It just doesn't sound good no matter how you look at it.

We definitely don't have it as bad as Japan. These poor people have been hit with so many disasters that I don't see how they can go on. This is truly a horrific mess. The earthquakes are so bad, not counting the tsunami. The death toll is rising drastically, my heart pours out to their misfortune. The flooding and destruction of their cities is just terrible. Now they have to deal with these Nuclear Power Plants that is emitting radiation and starting to affect a lot of people. No one should have to experience such disasters as this. Japan needs help very badly.

It will be hard for the United States to give a lot of aide because we are broke. There is a limit to how much we can do for them. Although we owe them money, we must hope that they will decrease our debt to them for us coming forward to help them. Let's face it; it will be expensive for everyone involved. Because of Japan's disaster, it is going to affect the United States in many ways. The cost of everything coming from Japan will go up. This could raise the price of toys right on up to gasoline. This not only is hell for Japan but we are going to feel their misfortune also.

Its bad enough our Country has to fear the Terrorist's that want to bring harm to our Country. But now we have an economic Terrorist that wants to cause instability within our economy. Rumor has it that a man named Stephon Lerner who is a labor leader and possibly works for S.E.I.U., however there is no proof that he works for them, but no one will deny it. And to top it all off the Whitehouse won't comment on it either. He has been caught giving a speech involving turning our economy up side down. He wants to crash the New York Stock Exchange and convince thousands of people to quit making their mortgage payments. Why is this man planning the destruction of America?

What is up? This kind of Terrorism is scarier than can be imagined. If he would succeed with his plan, we all could be in trouble. We must not become a victim of the Union leader's ideas and their future plans for America. The Unions are so corrupt and are hurting for money because they have lost a lot of members, which makes them desperate and dangerous. There has been an incident where the Unions have been accused of putting plastic cockroaches into people's food trying to convince us and pressure us in to believing that things like this wouldn't happen if the company serving the food was supported by the Unions. This is just another ploy to get new members that will give them more money.

The Unions are causing more chaos and trying to hurt America. We must not let this happen. This kind of behavior would explain why Andy Stern visits the Whitehouse as much as he does. It's amazing to watch everything that goes on in the Whitehouse. We should wonder why Obama feels the need to associate with Andy Stern. I bet as an American you weren't aware of the fact that many of our laws are decided because of the Unions. It's too bad that Obama picks and chooses which laws to enforce, sounds like too much favoritism to me.

The Unions also have been accused of prank telephone calls to a Governor, as they impersonated someone else; just to cause more problems for the Governor. It seems there is no end to what they will do to get what they want. We must beware of the Union leaders because they will go to any extreme when their money starts slipping through their fingers from lack of membership. They won't roll over and disappear; a decrease in funds will create real monsters. They need to realize that using scare tactics in politics can backfire.

As we all know that majority of the population wants us to drill for oil on our shorelines and not elsewhere. We all need to hold on to our undies because Obama is selling us out. Just recently he told the Brazilian people that he will support and pay over 2 billion dollars for them to drill on their shoreline. Just what the hell is going on? We are now going to pay Brazil to drill for oil? I truly think that Obama has lost it. This man has made some of the worst decisions in history, and this one is probably the biggest so far.

We are not only paying them to drill, but Obama says we will be their number one customer. So let's get this right. We are going to invest in them and pay for their oil drilling and then we are going to buy our oil from them. What the hell is wrong with Obama? It is time and I repeat this, it is time we quit wasting all our money and drill on our own shorelines and to hell with the other Countries. Why is this so easy for 60% of the population to figure out and yet the Whitehouse and Capital Hill can't? I can't help but to wonder how much money Obama is going to make on this ridiculous decision. By us doing this we will be creating more jobs in Brazil. What happened to the U.S.A.? Here goes more of our tax payer dollars to another Country. This really sucks... I know that I and millions of others do not want to develop Brazil's oil reserves at our expense.

On the news the other day they stated that the government is trying to get more people to go on welfare. Why? Did you ever hear of such a thing? It could very well be true. The government can't get enough control until we the people have to rely on them for everything.

The more people on welfare or state aid, makes it a little easier for them to handle us.

Our government has stated many times that they are about to shut down because of lack of funds to run our Country. They continue to have a meeting of the minds to decide what to do to keep the government going. With this being said why has our government just given the rebels in Libya, 25 million dollars worth of uniforms, tents, body amour and food? This is unacceptable. Just why would we fork out this kind of money to another Country when we are in a financial crisis and can barely afford to keep our own government up and running? What the hell is wrong with our politicians? Their nuts!!

Our government can not expect us to tolerate everything they dish out. If the truth be known, this book could go on and on and never have an ending. These chapters are a wake up call about the issues that are going on right now, what about all the issues and laws that we haven't heard about yet? This sounds a little scary, don't you think?

Chapter 22 .... Year 2025

My name is Tom Willis, it is now the year 2025 and we are no longer a free Nation. The government has taken control over all of us. They have destroyed our desire to live. Each day begins a new struggle. Our existence is all there is. We walk, talk, sleep, work and eat when they tell us to. Every thought we have is a muffled vision within our self. If it weren't for my wife Ellie and my daughter Lisa along with our son Eric, I would probably loose my mind.

As my family and I sat down to dinner, such as it was, we try to discuss things that will brighten our day. Ellie and I were discussing how we use to sit down and watch movies and munch on candy bars, then my daughter asked "daddy what is a candy bar?" I choked back the tears as I tried to explain to her, what a chocolate candy bar was and how it tasted. All I could think about was how terrible, my little girl does not know what a candy bar is. With that thought in mind, a tear rolled down my cheek. As I wiped it off I just didn't know what to say to her. How can you describe the taste to some one if they have never experienced it? I begin to tell her about the sugar and chocolate inside and how it really tasted sweet and very good. Lisa looked at me with her big brown eyes and said "why can't I have a candy bar? Then Eric said "me too". So I explained that the government has decided that sugar was not good for us and they will not sell it any more. Of course that wasn't quite what two kids wanted to hear. Lisa said "that is stupid". "We should be able to have a candy bar too." I told her that I agreed but we had no choice in the matter. Then I insisted she eat her green beans and rice. But I could not blame her at all, because I too was sick of rice.

Every Monday we had to stand in a very long line just to get food. It always varied but was never enough to feed the four of us. Sometimes we would get milk, bread and meat. But it was always rice, vegetables and dried fruit. Oh yes there was always a twelve pack of water. It had been so long since I had a cup of coffee that I have almost forgotten what it tasted like. The lawmakers had some damn excuse about the caffeine in it and it was not good for us. I used to ask myself why they don't let us have decaffeinated. But you could not argue with these people. They just would not listen to us.

During the winter months which used to be the holidays, we sometimes got a bag of oranges or apples. The kids just loved them. Christmas was a holiday you were not allowed to talk about. Ellie and I did, but it was forbidden. We sure miss Christmas; it was such a beautiful time of the year. It was nice to see everyone singing Christmas carols and looking at the pretty wrapped presents. I still have the ring Ellie bought me one year. She has worn out all the clothes that I had bought her, but she still had a necklace that she wore everyday. We don't talk about Christmas but we do celebrate it in our own way. It still has a place in our heart. We spend the day playing with the kids and just making it a special day. They of course don't know it is the holiday, they can take it away from us but it is still in our hearts and memories. Now that the kids are older I would love for them to experience the bright lights and watch them open their presents. I can not tell you how terrible it is now. There is no meaning to anything. It is just a day like any other. Ellie and I were so upset when they did away with all the holidays. It even hurt worse when they took away our right to pray and believe in God. If you were found praying or discussing any religion or holiday, it was automatic jail time. And believe me that place they call jail is terrible.

It is so hard to explain to the kids the way life used to be. But we are glad that we had them before they passed the new law that you could no longer get pregnant. If anyone was pregnant, their pregnancy was terminated. It didn't stop women from getting pregnant, but they had to go to the abortion clinic and abort it. I know someone who managed to hide her swollen stomach and actually had the baby. But weeks later they came and took the baby away. The government wants to decrease the population so they don't have to take care of so many people. We often wonder what happens to the babies they take from their parents, but it's just not a good thing to ask questions about.

My mother died 3 years ago with cancer. She didn't have to die, but our dear leaders refuse to give any medical help or medication to any one over 60 years of age. So each day she was alive was very painful for her. It was so hard to watch my mother cry and sob from the pain. I wanted so badly to help her, but if I did in any way then I was taken from my family for weeks at a time. There was a time we use to be able to get help and medication for what ailed us. But now even if you're younger, the wait is so long that it's not worth it. My brother once waited 6 months to get in to see a Doctor when he broke his leg. By the time he saw him, his leg was already healed in a deformed way, so it either had to be broken again and reset and a cast put on or just live with it.

There are only six Doctors in 200 square miles, and there are probably a million people in this area. My wife and I just don't know what to do anymore. Life seems so useless. The only thing they did not take away from us was our furniture and TV. The only problem is they control everything we watch. Sometimes there are movies on, but you can bet your sweet ass it is edited by them. Ellie and Eric don't get to go to school anymore like we used to. Their schooling is on the TV. Every day for 3 hours they get assignments and they work off the computer to do them and e-mail them in. But they control that also. You can't get on it now and surf the Web. All you can do is go to Web sites that are either political or educational. You can't e-mail a friend or listen to music. They do have a talk show that is kind of good, but again it is all put on by the government. If it could be fun or interesting they will not let you watch it.

Ellie and Eric are complaining again about how cold the house is. They did away with our thermostats. All homes are hooked up to some kind of wireless remote like system and they control our heat. We don't have to pay for heat, but I would rather pay for it than have them control it, because it is to cold in our house during the winter months. I liked it better when we could go to the thermostat and set it for the temperature we wanted.

Our paychecks are a joke. The employer you work for sends in all the money you made during that weeks pay period to the government. Then we get paid 20% of our check, what ever that may be. Last week my check was only $60.00. They expect us to live on that kind of money a week for a family of four. Although they do pay for our health insurance, housing, heat, food and utilities, it still is a struggle to live. They use to get the 20% out of our check and now we get the 20%.

All luxuries have been taken away. It really is disheartening to live. Everyday we wake up depressed. Our spirit has been broken and we find it hard to go on. It seems we do not have anything to look forward to. I use to be into hunting and looked forward to the seasons to open. We would eat deer, turkey, and grouse and if I was quick enough with my shot, I would get a rabbit. Ellie did a great job at cooking wild game. But now the government has raided all our homes and taken away our guns. We can no longer hunt for our meat or even protect ourselves.

Any desires we once had are gone. There are no chances to better yourself or to get ahead because are lawmakers won't let us. We might as well be puppets, because all we do is exist and do what were told. I have always been a strong willed man and have always had no fear taking care of my family. But times have changed now and I am beginning to loose my will to live. How terrible this must sound, but once a man's spirit has been broke and there is no light at the end of the tunnel, then what the hell is the use. We absolutely hate our lives and the more they take away from us the harder it is to survive. Suicide sounds like a cop out, but Ellie and I can't continue to live under the ruling of our changed Nation. It has not gotten to that point yet, but it could be our only choice.

Tomorrow brings another day to go to work. I am hoping I have enough gas in my car to get there. The gas prices just dropped from $6.99 a gallon to $6.79 a gallon. I can usually go to work 2 days on a gallon of gas. But it cost us so much money for gas out of my $60.00 pay check. The gas was up to $9.59 a gallon, but when people weren't showing up for work because of lack of money for gas, they finally dropped the prices. After all, they don't get any of our money if we don't show up for work, so they try to make sure that we have just enough money for us to get to work.

I can remember back about two years ago, when about a thousand people decided to rebel against the system and not work. That was a disaster, because for those who chose not to work, they turned off their heat and quit giving them any food. I wanted to join in with them but I feared the outcome, and I was glad I didn't go along with it. I would not want my wife and kids to suffer. They still have stores that sell food, but it is so expensive that there is no way you could afford to buy anything. Last year when Ellie had her birthday, I had a few bucks left so I decided to buy her some kind of cake. Of course you could only buy the sugar free and salt free products with no icing, but it was cake. I could only afford to buy her a package of Twinkies for $8.00. I found some old candles and put a candle in one of the Twinkies. I still remember how she broke down and cried. I was hoping it was because of my kindness and thoughtfulness. I am sure it was. But just living as we live brings tears to your eyes.

Ellie and I were talking about the political issues that we heard on the TV, when Lisa decided to run up to the TV and slap it like she was mad at it. I asked her what she was doing, and she stated "Daddy isn't that the bad man that you said wouldn't let us have candy bars?" I had to laugh because she was right. It was our World leader. At one time we had a President for each Country, but they did away with that position and made one man in charge of the whole World. We now have a Vice President for each Country. It's just a mess. To top it all off, our world leader can barely speak English let alone rule our World.

I guess because we owed China so much money, China basically took over the whole World and became the ruler of the Universe. Boy did that suck. Now here I am a true American and some foreigner is telling us what to do. This is why many of us can not stand our lives or our situations that created this rotten existence that is called living.

It was the year 2018 when our world as we once knew it was gone. How we have lived like this for seven years I will never know. Will we make another seven years? I really doubt it. I can see that things will not get better, but perhaps worse as time goes on. I do wonder how it could get worse, but then ten years ago I would have never imagined this.

This all started when an African American named Barack Obama became President. Ellie and I were very glad we did not vote for him. We felt we just could not trust him, and we were right. He totally destroyed our Country and left us all in a mess. It was because of him and his ideas and excessive spending of money that caused our Country to fail. He only served one term of four years, but what a ride. America took a chance on electing Obama to be our Commander in Chief. However, many felt there was hope for change and better things to come. Well we got change and then more change and before we knew it, America was no longer the land of the free; it became a Nation of slaves. It was almost like it was a pay back to the white man from hundreds of years ago when African Americans were slaves. Although at that time, I'm sure it was a terrible thing to happen to the blacks, but after all this is the millennium and things like that just don't happen like back in the barbaric days. Still, many of us feel it is a plan that was put into play many years ago and now implemented by Obama. Who really knows?

But Ellie and I do know that our Country was fine, not perfect, but it functioned and worked for the American people. As you can already determine, that Obama did not make another term, nor did a majority of the Senate and House members either. When a new President took over in 2012, things begin to look up and many things were changing back like they use to be. What a relief it was to have someone in office that would listen to us and be concerned with our wants and needs. When Obama was President he would not listen to anyone. He just made up the rules as he went along, he lied, he bribed and he did what ever he wanted to, including going against the Constitution.

The President after him did so well that he got reelected for a second term. Things were back to normal, or so we thought. The darkest of all days came when China decided they wanted all the trillions of dollars back and demanded payment at once. I guess China was having a few financial problems of their own and wanted their money. It was impossible for our Nation to come up with that kind of money. After several meetings of the minds with China, they could not come to any agreement. China then threatened us with war.

Our President was put into a terrible spot and knew there was no way out except war. We increased our military troops, began another draft system and prepared for war. As China watched us prepare to retaliate, they decided war was not the answer to solve their money problems. After one more meeting, the decision was made to let China become the World leader and our President was to step down to Vice President and so on until the chain of command was altered. All of Congress was dismissed, except for a few that filled other positions. This is when our Nation lost its freedom and our rights. Then each and every day there was new demands and new concessions and before we knew it, we woke to being a slave of our Nation. I realize this was just a quick summary of all the events that took place in the last few years, but life as we once knew it has now disappeared and all we're left with is memories of what it was like and who was responsible for this outcome.

Mr. Obama made history, as a cruel, arrogant leader who lost our Nations freedom and put mankind into jeopardy. We often wonder what has happened to him. We heard once that he was in China trying to weasel his way into their political system. Ellie and I still think he was in on this with China in the first place. But who are we, just some peons trying to survive the new world.

Summary

My dear fellow Americans, the time has come for us to take back our Nation. We must choose the right person for office. Most importantly we must study their background and judge them by the people they associate with and their commitment to wanting a better and free Nation. If we want our freedom restored, we must do our homework. We need to abolish all Progressive and Communist traits. We have an obligation to our Country and our children's future to make America a free Nation once again.

We have tried to be heard and have been ignored. The next step is for us to take action. We can not use violence because it will give them ammunition to take over more control of us. The next best thing would be our minds. We must be smarter than them and have quicker wits about us. We must not let them manipulate us or our Nation.

Do we want to loose our freedom and liberty, no of course not? So let freedom be our leader and our guide. We should not have to worry about our Country and the shape it's in. But now it is our responsibility to transform America back, back to a more comfortable and righteous Nation. Those of you, who think America is just fine, you need to take a better look at what is happening around you, and regroup. The majority of Americans are concerned and upset.

We the people of the United States demand respect and understanding from our government. We receive none, because of that, we are choosing to elect some one with good traits, conservative ways and a high priority in the moral department to better our Nation and free it from despair.

Please know this; we can not accept Social Justice as our way of living. We will not allow its existence among us. We like our freedom, our liberty and justice, but do not want it controlled by our government. They can only control the things that we let them. So let's remember that. The key word here is, let them. We must take away their rights to our future endeavors.

We have seen what a Progressive leader can do, and we don't like it. We do not want Health Care or Cap & Trade. And the big problem is, spending all this money that our lawmakers continue to do. We can not go on spending like this and not expect some kind of bad results. By spending all our money and cutting back on military issues, we can expect our Country to become weak. We have always been a strong Nation and now we could be in danger. We must ask this question; what is Obama up to? Why does he lie, sneak around and hide important information that is a necessity to Congress's voting decisions? You can not take away our money, lessen our military options and manipulate all housing and financial systems without causing chaos and grief.

We don't want Socialism, Communism or Progressivism ruling our World. It never works out and we the people are always the ones who are abused by its existence. I for one do not want to be told what to do or when I can do it. We should be able to eat and say what we want. We want our America back, and it is up to us to take it back. It can be projected that the majority of us will retaliate.

Rumor has it that our government would like to strip us of our guns. But because they know we are to strong for this measure to take effect, they are going to raise the price of ammo and make it hard to buy. Gee, what good is a gun without ammo? That's what they want, putting us in another helpless situation.

We want to be able to use our weapons, after all who is going to protect us from our own government? As each month goes by, Congress gets more and more crooked. We have all the reasons in the world not to trust our government. They have proven that to us over and over again.

For those of you, who voted for Obama, shame on you, I realize you have been educated by him since his inaugural speech. It is true, he is deceiving and has many tricks up his sleeve, so I can see how some of you got drawn in to his Socialistic web. Just think before you vote on the next person to take office. If we don't do this right, we will all be in a world of trouble and our rights and liberty will be gone and you can **Kiss Freedom Goodbye..**

We all want back to normal. Since Obama was elected, the Nation has been in turmoil. He tries to move to fast so that we can't catch up with what his next agenda will be. But wait Mr. Obama we will let you know what's on our agenda, and that is to get your ass out of our Whitehouse. Take your family and your Social Progressive ways and be gone.

It will be easier to get Obama out of office, than his side kicks. As you know, the Democrats have been siding with Obama since he's been in office. So we need to relieve them of their positions also. We need to concentrate on removing Pelosi and Reid. Those two are bad news and need to go. Rumor has it in California that they just love Pelosi, but that comment just rubbed me the wrong way. How can you love some one who is a control freak? This woman will bring harm to our Nation with stupidity and Progressiveness. She is an instigator and loves to rub our noses in any bill that is passed that we the people do not want. She is trouble.

Sometimes my mind runs rampart and I worry about the possibility of a shortage in food. Then it worries me to think that if a war broke out that our military would not be strong enough to handle it. As more thoughts tip toe through my brain, the thought of no heat in the winter months tends to scare me, because the price of fuels will be rocketing sky high. Then what about our health, will we be too old for them to consider giving us surgery or healing what ails us? What if it's a terminal illness and time is critical and surgery is needed, it could be the difference between life and death. By the time you add these worries up; it's damn scary and feels like we have lost control of our own life. It will be like this for all of us, if we continue to let our government rule the roost.

We should not have to worry about these kinds of things. Life is stressful enough without worrying about what the government's next move will be. You can best believe that they are not done with us yet. What about our children, how will they survive in a world powered by Socialist and Communist? It will be hell on earth for them, so we must also fight for the rights of our children.

No more earmarks or pork spending. Each bill that is up for a vote will be about one thing only. When the Health Care Bill was ready to be voted on; they also through in the Student Loan take over. So if you voted for Health Care than the Student Loan Program would automatically be voted on also. This must stop. The only reason Congress does this is because they are too lazy to debate on, or sign numerous bills. Voting on these bills is part of their job, and they should have to read each bill before signing them. Every Congress person should know exactly what is in a bill before they vote on it. We should be able to say to one of them; what is in the bill? They should be able to tell us all about it. They make way too much money for them to be ignorant of a bill. This is their job and they are not doing a good job, so out they go. In with the new and out with the old.

America I am telling you now that we are in severe trouble if we do not change the line up in the Whitehouse. Obama is connected to many outside companies and he uses our Nation to distribute the money he needs to fulfill his commitments with these other people.

The fact that our government is not functioning properly is of the utmost importance. If any of us were working for a company and we failed to do our job correctly, we would be fired. The same should be for Congress. They get away with so much, that it is incredible, is it possible for them to get away with murder before they actually get what's coming to them?

We should fear our government because they are sneaky and they can't be trusted. Obama continues to blame Bush for our problems, only because he does not want to accept the fact that he is our problem. All President's do something we Americans don't like but Bush never went against our wishes on purpose, nor did he tease and taunt us because of what we desire.

Any and all bills that Obama has signed should become null and void. We can not continue to have a government that is so unstable and unreliable. The idea of getting to see the President has always been exciting and rewarding for the American people. However, now we could care less if we see or hear him because he has done us wrong. We do not want another Hitler ruling our World and ending our life style as we know it.

Have you ever seen a President do the opposite of what we the people want? It has to be on purpose, because what other reason would there be? Our President is supposed to be our leader and our mentor, not a jerk who ignores the people. This is an astounding situation that just keeps getting worse. Each day that passes keeps us in wonder of just what will happen next? How many other bills will he try to push through office before his term is up? He is going against our Constitutional rights and we must appeal all his devious actions.

Americans love to eat. We must be able to have any choice of food we desire, not what the government wants us to eat. My dear fellow Americans, does this seem right to you? Are you truly happy with the government controlling us?

The following, is a list of things that our government is going to control in one way, shape or form.

☺ Taxing foods that are bad for us, or not allowing us to eat them or make them available to us.

☺ Health Care that the government will control and decide if your worthy of treatment.

☺ A Cap & Trade bill that will raise the costs of our utilities bills, which will be so expensive, that many people will freeze to death because they can't afford to pay their heating bill. Plus your house will have to have a license posted in it, that it is energy efficient. You won't be able to sell your house until the energy efficiency has been brought up to the government's new code standard. Which will cost us so much money, we will not be able to ever sell our home. Each year this license will have to be renewed, costing us more money yet. How many of us can afford all new windows, furnace's or roof's?

☺ Controlling student loans and deciding which college they will let you attend. The choice will be theirs, not yours. We as taxpayers will have to foot the bill for all college fees.

☺ A Carbon Tax will be implemented to tax the air we breathe and how much carbon you put out when driving to work, and there will be a mileage charge.

☺ Value added tax that will be so high you won't be able to buy anymore luxuries.

☺ The smokers will be restricted from enjoying a smoke out in public.

☺ Religion will become obsolete. You will no longer be able to express your views or say a prayer.

☺ The holidays will not be honored any more. They will be a thing in the past.

☺ TV and radio shows will be edited by our government for our viewing pleasure.

☺ Swearing in public will be a crime. Tell me; if your boat tipped over with all you're belonging's in it, wouldn't you say a few choice words?

☺ Your medical history will be displayed on a Web site for any one to see.

☺ Social Security will either be taken away or we will take a cut in pay, due to the government spending of all our funds.

☺ Our taxes will rise so high, there will be very little for us to live on.

☺ The government will be able to take away our land and our home through Eminent Domain, if the government wants to.

☺ Individuals who want children will have to get an okay from our government, because they want to control the population.

☺ Ammunition will be scarce or priced so high we can't afford to buy it.

☺ Taxes will be higher for everything, whether you are tanning or buying Insurance.

The time has come to send Congress a message, by voting everyone out. I can not stress enough, how important this is to our future. We owe it to ourselves and our children to better our system and clean house. Have you ever cleaned your house and sat back and looked at it? Its shinny and clean and just makes you feel better. That is how we will all feel when we get rid of the jerks in the Whitehouse and on Capital Hill.

There are so many places to cut expenses that it is hard to believe that not one of our Representatives has pushed to do so. Who are they afraid of? What are they afraid of? You see there are so many deals and money exchanging hands, that it would be hard to answer those questions.

We all know that our Nation is in trouble and needs our help. Why can't we fire them all and elect the new back into office? Where does it say that we can't do that? If a person can make a citizens arrest, then why can't we relieve these people from office?

Please know this fellow Americans, we can do this, we have to do this and we will do this. Our future is at stake, and we must take the time to make adjustments for our society. We must fire our government and replace it with Conservative individuals that want to better our future and be concerned with our concerns. We can not make the mistake of ignoring this problem with our government or we will be sorry.

My husband and I always have the American flag hung in our yard. One day we were winterizing the yard and picking things up to store from the inclement weather soon to be coming, as I was taking down the flag, it touched the ground, and my husband lost it. He told me that I can never let that happen again. To my surprise, he shocked me; he felt that was not acceptable to let our flag touch the ground. Wow, what a true American. And yes, those were the exact words that went through my head. I can honestly say he loves his Country and finds much disappointment in the events that are taking place. I guess that is how a good Marine feels. It did not bother me at the time. But with respect for him and my Country, I have never let it happen again.

Politics never were a big deal for me. I voted and watched the news and did what most Americans do. But, back a year ago I had open heart surgery. While being home recovering and healing, I had no other choices but to watch TV. It was bombarded with news shows, mostly political. As I listened, I realized that our Country is not doing real well. So I began to pay more attention and became more concerned as I heard all the political views. It made me angry, mad and worried. It was like, what the hell is wrong with our government? I wanted to do something about it. But as we all know, a one man team can never win. I just wanted to make a difference, a good difference. I can only hope that many-many Americans feel the same way.

It is strange to have a different outlook, than you had ever had before. As a hair salon owner and operator, I chat with lots of people and can not believe that the majority of people I converse with have no idea of what is going on in our government. I find it hard to believe that our citizens' are in the dark, like I use to be. That is what inspired me to write this book. I want everyone to know how much trouble we are in and how it could get a lot worse if we don't pay more attention to our government's actions. With that being said, Please wake up America and smell the roses, because we are going on a ride to hell if we don't make an attempt to resolve the crime in the Whitehouse and on Capital Hill.

I will say that many people do not believe that anything bad can happen to us. These are the people that are in for a rude awakening. It will be a normal day today and tomorrow our rights, freedom and liberty will diminish and slip away. We must love and cherish our rights. We have the right to voice our opinions and warn the ignorant of what could be coming. For those of you who are Obama lovers, you have no idea what is about to happen to your life. For those of you who are not paying attention to what is going on well bless your souls because our world is about to be swept out from under us.

If you like being taken care of by the government and you choose to let them rule your world, than you need to cowboy up and be a real American. You're just as bad as our leader and even worse, because you're a leech, and have no desires or wants of your own.

We, as Americans must stand up and fight for our rights, because once there gone, they are gone forever, and we can **Kiss Freedom Goodbye**.

Our economy is in sad shape, Our military is being forced to cut back, the government has become crooked and is neglecting our rights as a citizen, along with many new laws being shoved down our throats. The worse thing in this whole world would be to keep spending money, but that's all our government knows how to do. We need individuals that have a back bone and know what to do to save America. We can just ignore the situation and maybe it will get better on its own, but do you really think that will happen?

Through all these years, our Constitution has been our guide and our strength to maintain an even keel in society. Our leaders today do not and will not accept this book of laws, as being our guide to a free Nation. We did not elect these people to rewrite the Constitution, but to honor its purpose and meaning in regards to a fair and just system.

Thanks to our founding fathers, they knew what could happen with out some kind of system so we should be honored that back in those days they could foresee our future needs. The Constitution has been our political bible for many years. It is disappointing to realize that the government feels that they do not have to abide by it. This should be a solid clue that our President and majority of Congress is not interested in the American way and do not deserve to hold any office as a representative for the United States of America. It is that cut and dried. We, as true Americans do not want this kind of government.

I beg your attention to the above mentioned items and can only hope that many of you will be very adamant in regards to the dismissal of our government. Every day that we waste or hesitate, will give them another day to create more vicious bills and take more rights and money from us. Let us stop them before our children are slaves to a Nation run by Communists and Socialists.

The government is about to impose massive tax hikes on us. It will hurt us very badly. Majority of the population in the middle class live week to week for a paycheck. Many can not afford to loose another dime out of their pockets or they will not be able to pay their own debt.

If we want to survive this financial crisis that the government has put us in, then we have to get them out of office. It will be our only salvation. We would actually be better off with someone inexperienced, so they learn as they go and can't get into any trouble on their journey as President.

How many of us are willing to go to jail because of our beliefs? Not because you want to start trouble or riots, but because you don't want to abide by their new laws. Laws that hinder our every move and force us to do or buy something we don't want. Things are going to get rough for all of us. Even the rich will be complaining that they are paying too much. The middle class will become the lower class. The lower class as we know them now, will be guided and led around like a herd of sheep under the wings of the government, they will be fed, clothed and housed and loose all their rights and freedom.

We must not let this happen to us because of a group of dictators who were elected into office. We have learned and will become stronger in our views because of this. We will win to keep our rights, our freedom and our Nation from the perils of a bad government. We should believe what Glen Beck says when he states that "Faith, Hope and Charity" will save us all. We all must have faith that things will be better. We will all hope that each and every American wakes up and makes the right decisions in their voting choices. Americans have always been the most charitable people on earth. I have faith in the American people. There's hope that everyone will become smarter and wiser to our evil government. We all want to stand tall once again and be known as America, the land of the free.

Although it will be a struggle we must prepare ourselves for the worst. Once the government has run out of money and resources to operate and make our Country secure, then we the people will be on our own. The government officials will spend their time trying to save themselves and will not be concerned with us citizens.

It will be up to us to scurry for food and find other sources to live by. We must save some food for a later date. Buying extra's of canned goods, such as canned meats, vegetables, rice, flour, sugar, water, candles and any thing that might help you sustain life for a period of six months. Times could get very hard. We must struggle to help ourselves, as there will be no help from our government. It will be every man for him self.

There is a possibility that the government could stop all programs such as food stamps, Social Security, Disability, and any other programs that are linked to them. This would be a major disaster for the American people. But with the government spending too much money this is a possible threat. I hope I am wrong. I want to be wrong about all of this.

If you are living in a city, things will be worse for you. The chaos and rioting will be life threatening for you. The rural areas will be a safer place to be. But if the government does fail us, then no where will really be safe. Our food prices are soaring; our gas prices are rising weekly. Something is going to happen, mark my words.

For the record; I do like Barack Obama, but feel his decisions have harmed our Nation and because of this, we will suffer severe repercussions. This isn't a prediction, this is a present fact.

Soon our freedom of speech will be denied and Americans will not be able to express their thoughts like I have in this book. It bothers me to think that our future could hold tremendous problems that none of us can imagine, and yes this is a prediction.

It is time for us all to join together before it's too late, time is short. This is America's wake up call. We mustn't **Kiss Freedom Goodbye.**

Freedom for all and Good Luck to us!!!!!!

America the Land of the Free?

Goodbye Obama

Isn't it time for you to be leaving?
So we Americans can quit grieving.

We've tried, We've cried.
And yet all you do is deny.

We want our Freedom, it's our right.
Please don't make us get up and fight.

To see you go will be a delight.
A better future for us is in sight.

You have taunted us and teased.
Believe me were not pleased.

Going against our Constitution is unjust.
Getting you out of office is a must.

Our money is gone and all has been spent.
You have left us nothing, not even a cent.

All the bail-outs and the bribes.
Has awakened our Nations tribes.

You have made many promises and lied to us.
Now you're wondering what's the fuss.

As our Commander in Chief,
You have become a real thief.

You're trying to steal our rights and money.
And we don't think it's very funny.

Your all for the foreigners and have taken their side.
What's up with you that you take it in stride?

Goodbye Obama that stands in our way.
This is America and still is to this day!

The opinions and comments you have read
are solely that of the Author and previously
reported News Broadcasts and hopefully
shared by a majority of Americans who will
take to heart these words as knowledge.

If anyone is interested in commenting on **Kiss Freedom
Goodbye** or have some ideas you would like to share
with the Author, please feel free to send them to:

Ms. Cheryl Roote
P.O. Box 44
Barryton, Michigan 49305-0044